READING INSTRUCTION
FOR THE GIFTED

READING INSTRUCTION
FOR THE GIFTED

By

DONALD C. CUSHENBERY, Ed.D.

Professor of Education
University of Nebraska at Omaha
Omaha, Nebraska

CHARLES C THOMAS • PUBLISHER
Springfield • Illinois • U.S.A.

Published and Distributed Throughout the World by

CHARLES C THOMAS • PUBLISHER

2600 South First Street

Springfield, Illinois 62794-9265

© *1987 by* CHARLES C THOMAS • PUBLISHER

ISBN 0-398-05332-4

Library of Congress Catalog Card Number: 87-1897

Printed in the United States of America
SC-R-3

Library of Congress Cataloging in Publication Data

Cushenberry, Donald C.
    Reading instruction for the gifted.

    Bibliography: p.
    Includes index.
    1. Gifted children--Education--United States--Reading.
I. Title.
LC3993.5.C88   1987   371.95'3   87-1897
ISBN 0-398-05332-4

To my many colleagues during the past forty-two years who have identified gifted students and skillfully taught them to appreciate the importance of reading in their daily lives.

PREFACE

Gifted students have been a part of the total school population for hundreds of years; however, the identification and careful instruction of these learners is a somewhat recent trend in the public and private schools of America. For many years, some able learners were merely assigned additional work to complete in order to keep him and her "busy." As noted in this important volume, there are currently many local, state, and national programs for the gifted which are producing outstanding results, especially in the area of reading instruction.

Since many gifted and able pupils have a potential for becoming future community leaders, it is important for teachers at all learning levels to develop an educational program that provides for the careful identification and instruction of these learners. Special programs should be undertaken to help insure that each student reaches his or her potential level in the area of reading instruction. Parents and educators have a profound responsibility for working together cooperatively to maximize skill growth, especially in the language arts and particularly in reading.

This volume has been prepared to be an easy-to-read, authoritative source of teacher-tested suggestions that correlate with the latest research findings and relate to the overall curriculum of a school system. Teachers at all grade and learning levels should find the program descriptions and lesson plans to be applicable for many different kinds of school settings.

Chapter I defines the characteristics of gifted learners and presents some practical strategies for identifying these types of pupils. A historical overview of gifted education as well as careful descriptions of current exemplary programs for the gifted are contained in Chapter II. Chapters III, IV, and V contain a broad treatise of the most practical and significant teaching methods to help gifted readers improve their reading skill competencies. An extensive discussion of the principles and purposes of evaluation and a description of effective reading evaluation tools and strategies are included in Chapter VI. An important series of appendices present valuable data relating to such important aspects as periodicals for teachers, instructional materials, and professional books for teachers.

ACKNOWLEDGMENTS

The author wishes to acknowledge his indebtedness to the many faculty members and students in the Department of Teacher Education at the University of Nebraska at Omaha for their constant encouragement while the manuscript was in the process of preparation.

Appreciation is expressed to Mrs. Elaine Westbrook for her help in preparing the appendices and proofreading various chapters. Mrs. Becky Schnabel deserves a "thank you" for acting as the official courier for the author. Dr. Virginia Bryg, reading specialist of the Omaha Public Schools, is to be commended for her help with respect to her constructive evaluation of the total manuscript.

Sincere appreciation is extended to Mrs. Jan Wiebe, the manuscript typist, for her efficient and dedicated work. Her suggestions for certain changes in the various subsections helped considerably. The permission of Mr. Duane Webb of Sopris West, Incorporated, of Longmont, Colorado to utilize several pieces of material from EDUCATIONAL PROGRAMS THAT WORK is gratefully acknowledged. Ms. Elizabeth McCray, Project Director of the California Demonstration Program in Reading, Bakersfield, California, was a most informative source of information during my site visit to her classroom.

Further important visits were made at the McLean Elementary School in Wichita, Kansas. Special appreciation is extended to Mr. LaFever, Mrs. Milton, Ms. Johnson, and Ms. Wood of the McLean School for demonstrating efficient reading lessons with gifted pupils.

Finally, sincere gratitude is extended to Mr. Thomas Tollman, Chairman of the University of Nebraska at Omaha Library-Reference Department for his tireless assistance in locating important references.

CONTENTS

READING INSTRUCTION
FOR THE GIFTED

CHAPTER I

IDENTIFYING GIFTED STUDENTS IN YOUR CLASSROOM

One of the most challenging aspects of classroom instruction is to properly *identify* and *teach* those students who deviate from the norm to such a degree that they need special instruction. In the past, much attention has been given to the learning disabled, mentally handicapped, and physically deficient child with less attention directed to the gifted and talented pupil in many instances. Recently, some advocacy groups within the field of education have held meetings and published various papers to call attention to the importance of identifying and instructing those learners who have special talents.

At the present time most state departments of education have constructed innovative programs for instituting statewide projects for meeting the needs of gifted children. Many local school district officials have designed instructional plans for classroom teachers who instruct gifted children in all of the content areas; however, one very significant question has created a considerable amount of controversy—what criteria should be applied to *identify* gifted and talented students at the various grade levels?

In order to provide pertinent information about this significant aspect, the following major topics are discussed in this chapter: characteristics of gifted students; screening and identification strategies for the gifted; the use of commercial and informal instruments; and the value of related procedures in the identification process. A summary of the total chapter and a set of references conclude the chapter.

CHARACTERISTICS OF GIFTED STUDENTS

As noted earlier, there has been a considerable amount of debate and controversy among educators and the lay public regarding the definition and identification procedures which should be utilized with respect to pupils who appear to be especially bright and exhibit proficiencies which exceed those of the average learner. Though the construction of special programs for these children has received major attention in recent years, interest in educational activities for the gifted and creative is not new. Throughout history, recognition and encouragement have been dependent upon the nature of the gift and cherished beliefs existing at that time. The past and present provisions for these pupils have been unsystematic and inadequate.[1]

During the past twenty-five years, numerous authorities have offered lists of characteristics which they feel are descriptive of those learners who may be considered gifted. When studying the individual lists, one notes a sizable amount of agreement on several aspects of giftedness. In 1960, for example, Buhler and Guirl[2] compiled a checklist of representative characteristics which they felt all gifted children should possess. These aspects include the following:

1. High academic achievement
2. Advanced vocabulary and reading level
3. Expressive fine arts talent
4. Wholesome personal-social adjustment
5. Early physical competence
6. Superior intellectual ability
7. Effectively work independently
8. Persistent curiosity
9. Strong creative and inventive power
10. Special scientific ability
11. High energy level
12. Demonstrated leadership abilities
13. Well-developed mechanical skills

Eleven years later, the U.S. Commissioner of Education, Sidney P. Marland, directed a special study to determine a definition of identifying criteria for use with pupils who were thought to be gifted.[3] The summary statement indicated that the committee believed that children of high performance include those with demonstrated achievement and/or potential ability in any of the following areas, singly or in combination:

1. General intellectual ability
2. Specific academic aptitude
3. Creative or productive thinking
4. Leadership ability
5. Visual and performing arts
6. Psychomotor ability

At the present time nearly every state legislature in the United States has passed laws which mandate the identification of gifted and talented children and the establishment of special funding for such programs. Each state has the liberty and responsibility for determining the criteria to use for identifying those children with outstanding intellectual/academic abilities. According to Patricia Mitchell[4] of the National Association of State Boards of Education, officials have three basic issues which must be resolved: (1) whether to establish a broad or narrow definition of such pupils; (2) how to limit the number of children to be served; and (3) the appropriate use of national or local standards for comparing students. A narrow definition emphasizes only intellectual/academic abilities while a broad definition assumes that other characteristics are important such as leadership, creative thinking, and artistic expression in addition to intellectual and academic talents. The set of characteristics utilized is correlated closely with the amount of human and financial resources available in each state for such programs.

Some authorities prefer to cite the characteristics of gifted and talented pupils by the use of personal and social descriptors. Tuttle and Becker[5] developed a list of characteristics which they feel are typical of children with gifted ability:

1. Is curious
2. Is persistent in pursuit of interests and questions
3. Is perceptive of the environment
4. Is critical of self and others
5. Has a highly developed sense of humor, often a verbal orientation
6. Is sensitive to injustices on personal and worldwide levels
7. Is a leader in various areas
8. Is not willing to accept superficial statements, responses, or evaluations
9. Understands general principles easily
10. Often responds to the environment through media and means other than print and writing
11. Sees relationships among seemingly diverse ideas
12. Generates many ideas for a specific stimulus

In analyzing a composite list of characteristics of highly talented and gifted pupils, one may properly classify these aspects into at least five major categories: degree of creativity; leadership ability; musical, artistic, and dramatics characteristics; motivational tendencies; and learning descriptors. The section which follows contains definitive aspects for each of the categories.

A. *Degree of Creativity*

1. Exhibits much curiosity about the world around him/her and makes numerous inquiries about processes and products.

2. Produces numerous plausible answers and solutions which appear to be unique and innovative.
3. States a number of expressions of ideas and opinions which offer various solutions for everyday problems. The proposals appear to be far-reaching and extraordinary.

B. *Leadership Ability*

1. Demonstrates that he/she has excellent rapport with all classmates and appears to be held in high respect.
2. Shows a feeling of self-confidence when in the company of either peers or instructors. Conveys a feeling of good self-ego without attending arrogance or conceit.
3. Completes responsibilities in a prompt and efficient manner. Follows directions without additional explanations or substantiation. The final product is of the highest quality.

C. *Musical, Artistic, and Dramatics Characteristics*

1. Exhibits willingness to engage in school activities requiring a high level of musical, artistic, and/or dramatics ability.
2. Uses appropriate voice inflection and gestures to convey a given message to the audience.
3. Demonstrates a sustained interest in pursuing the goal of becoming the most able actor, artist, or actress possible.
4. Shows an appreciation for a broad scope of various kinds of music and art and is proficient in the knowledge and nature of these areas.

D. *Motivational Tendencies*

1. Conveys an absorbing interest in a large variety of topics and articles and seeks to learn how various aspects of such areas as science, social studies, and the humanities relate to each other.
2. Displays a tendency to actively pursue an assignment or task until it is completed correctly and on schedule.
3. Appears to be easily motivated when he or she understands the usefulness of the completion of a given task.

E. *Learning Characteristics*

1. Conveys evidence of a very advanced oral and written vocabulary for his/her grade and/or age level. Words and phrases are used in a meaningful way within a proper context when dealing with a sizable number of diverse subjects and topics.
2. Gives evidence of knowing many facts and concepts relating to a large number of varied topics in all of the major content areas such as social studies and sciences.
3. Demonstrates that mastery and later recall of facts and figures is an easy learning activity.

SCREENING AND IDENTIFICATION STRATEGIES FOR THE GIFTED

The procedures for identifying the gifted child have evolved considerably during the past five or six decades. Until about 1955, the typical procedure for identifying gifted children was the use of individual intelligence instruments combined with the results obtained from nationally known achievement tests. When it was not possible to utilize the services of a psychologist to administer an individual instrument, a group intelligence measure such as the *Lorge-Thorndike* or *California Test of Mental Maturity* was designated for obtaining a general measure of intelligence. Particular attention was given by teachers and administrators to the level and magnitude of the verbal score of the pupil. In most instances, an I.Q. score of at least 130 was necessary to be considered gifted; however, some school authorities insisted on a minimum score of 140. About 1960, several noted authorities undertook and completed several research studies which demonstrated that many other criteria besides I.Q. should be used in the identification of the gifted and talented. It was discovered that obtaining a *true* I.Q. score for some pupils was a difficult venture because of cultural and language barriers. Techniques involving structured observation techniques were developed which allowed the observer to evaluate such human traits as the ability to express new concepts; create new solutions with unusual components; and demonstrate effective closure in problem-solving situations. The data elicited from such techniques were combined with scores from intelligence and achievement measures to form the basis for helping determine the degree and extent to which a given pupil may be considered talented and gifted.

At the present time, there appears to be a heavy reliance placed on the scores of various commercial tests in combination with the data obtained from intelligence tests. Before any of these tests are employed, a *careful* study should be undertaken to determine the usefulness of a given instrument. The *Mental Measurements Yearbooks* and *Reading Tests and Reviews* should be consulted relating to the professional comments of test authorities regarding the value of a given instrument. Particular attention should be given to such aspects as validity, reliability, cost, and objectivity. Recommendations from other educators regarding the face validity of certain tests should be obtained. Because of the technical nature of certain instruments, some of them will have to be administered by professionals such as school psychologists and reading specialists.

The Use of Intelligence Instruments

One of the most frequently utilized instruments is the intelligence test. Individual tests such as the *Stanford-Binet Scale* and the *Wechsler Scales* are two of the most commonly used measures. The *Binet* (Riverside) was renormed in 1972 and evaluates subjects from the two-year-old through the superior adult level. Verbal and manipulative tasks are required such as noting the parts of the human body, following simple commands, and identifying various objects while other test items at the eighth year, for example, require the correct definitions of vocabulary words, noting verbal absurdities, and similarities and differences.

The *Wechsler Scales* (Psychological Corporation) comprise three different tests: *Wechsler Preschool and Primary Scale of Intelligence* (ages 4 to 6.5); *Wechsler Intelligence Scale for Children* (ages 6.5 to 16.5); and *Wechsler Adult Intelligence Scale* (ages 16 through adult). Each test consists of two scales: *verbal* and *performance*. The *verbal* scale entails such aspects as giving information; finding answers to oral arithmetic problems; and stating digits forward and backward. The performance section is composed of test items requiring the subject to arrange pictures in proper sequence; place sets of blocks in the same pattern as the one on the examiner's card; and put puzzle pieces together to form a picture.

In addition to the major individual tests just described, educators may choose from a number of group intelligence measures. These include the *Cattell Culture Fair Intelligence Test* (WPS); *Hemmon-Nelson Tests of Mental Ability* (Riverside); *Lorge-Thorndike Intelligence Tests, Multilevel Edition* (Riverside); and *Primary Mental Abilities Test* (S.R.A.).

When analyzing the I.Q. scores derived from either individual or group tests for the purpose of placement of children in gifted and talented classes, one must take into consideration a number of cautions. The most important aspects are as follows:

1. It is difficult, if not impossible, to arrive at a precise I.Q. score. The factor of standard error may suggest that any one derived score may deviate several points from the true score.
2. Because abilities differ considerably with respect to the level of maturity among elementary children, the goal of achieving a pre-

cise score may be quite difficult. Group intelligence instruments allow for even wider latitude.

3. Scores received from various intelligence tests tend to demonstrate much disparity because of the difference in skills being measured.
4. Educators have found that the determination of a valid I.Q. score is difficult for certain pupils because of such deficiencies as inadequate home environment, lack of motivation, language problems, and emotional and social maladjustments.

In summary, because of the lack of preciseness in an intelligence measurement, many other instruments and techniques should be utilized in the screening and identification processes for gifted and talented pupils.

Supplementary Tests for Screening

Depending on the views of the examiner or supervisor of special programs, further instruments such as those dealing with personality, learning abilities, and motor proficiency may yield additional data for making final decisions regarding the identification of special students. A sampling of the commercial tests and publishers in these categories include the following:

1. *Bruininks-Oseretsky Test of Motor Proficiency* is an individual test for measuring a subject's proficiency in gross, fine, and general motor components. (American Guidance)
2. *California Test of Personality* can be utilized from the kindergarten through college levels for assessing self and social adjustment as aspects of total personality. (C.T.B.)
3. *Children's Apperception Test* is used by psychologists for subjects ages 4–10 as a projective measure for evaluating total personality. (Psychological)
4. *Developmental Test of Visual-Motor Integration* is composed of various geometric forms for measuring visual perception and motor proficiency for subjects ages 2–15. (Follett)
5. *Differential Aptitude Tests* consist of a series of aptitude tests to help determine scholastic ability of older pupils in Grades 8–12. (Psychological)
6. *Lincoln-Oseretsky Motor Development Scale* for subjects from ages 6–14 is an individual test for evaluating several types of unilateral and bilateral motor skills. (Stoelting)
7. *Mills Learning Methods Test* is a valuable individual test for helping

to determine the best teaching approach to employ when planning lessons for certain pupils. (Mills)

8. *System of Multicultural Pluralistic Assessment* can be used with young children from ages 5–11 and is a major instrument for estimating the potential for learning on the part of the examinee. (Psychological)

9. *Thematic Apperception Test* is a projective test for the purpose of assessing personality patterns. (Psychological)

10. *Valett Developmental Survey of Basic Learning Abilities* analyzes a child's ability in the important areas of tactile, auditory, and visual discrimination as well as language development. (Consulting)

There are numerous achievement tests in reading and other areas which can serve as valuable resource tools for obtaining data which can be employed for the identification of gifted pupils. The following are representative tests which are used by many school district personnel for this and other purposes. (Some of these are described in greater detail in Chapter VI.)

1. *Brown-Carlsen Listening Comprehension Test* (Psychological) Grades 9–13
2. *California Reading Tests* (CTB) Grades 1–12
3. *Diagnostic Reading Tests* (Committee) Grades 1–College
4. *Iowa Tests of Basic Skills* (Riverside) Grades 1–9
5. *Nelson-Denny Reading Test* (Riverside) Grades 9–12
6. *School and College Ability Tests* (SCAT) (Addison) Grades 3–13
7. *Senior High Assessment of Reading Performance* (CTB) Grades 9–12
8. *Sequential Tests of Educational Progress* (Addison) Grades 3–12
9. *Wide Range Achievement Test* (Jastak) Grades K–College
10. *Woodcock Reading Mastery Tests* (A.G.S.) Grades K–12

When making use of the data from the previous tests, a determination needs to be undertaken regarding critical scores which are to be utilized for the screening process. If percentiles are employed, the decision to select only students who score at the 99th percentile or higher may be made. Other indices such as stanines or grade placements are sometimes considered as well. The gifted and talented student should score at a high level on a variety of these kinds of measures.

The Role of Informal Tests

No one commercial test can possibly include every facet of learning ability and thus must be supplemented by informal, teacher-made instruments. The data derived from such instruments as the reading interest inventory and the cloze technique can yield important evidence with respect to the extent of reading and language development which may be typical of the exceptionally bright learner. The following reading interest inventory may be constructed for use with most elementary and secondary students. The results of this instrument can lend valuable information regarding the depth and nature of a reader's interest.

Reading Interest Inventory

1. Name _____ Grade _____ School _____
2. Where do you secure most of the books you read for pleasure and entertainment?
   City library _____ Friends _____ Bookstores _____
   School library _____ Home library _____
3. Approximately how many complete books have you read during the past year? _____
4. Give the titles of three or four of the books you have read.
   _____　_____
   _____　_____
5. Do you have any hobbies? If so, what are they?
   _____
6. How many hours a week do you watch television? _____ Name two or three television shows you like the best. _____
   _____　_____
7. Have you visited any countries besides the United States? _____ If so, what are their names?
   _____
8. Do you read a newspaper on a regular basis? _____ If you do, what is the name of the newspaper?
   _____
9. Which of the following sections of the newspaper do you generally read?
   A. Sports section _____　　D. Feature stories _____
   B. Comics _____　　　　　　E. Want Ads _____
   C. Editorials _____　　　　　F. Other _____
10. If you had at least an hour of free time for reading each day, what kinds of reading material would you likely select? Why?
    _____
    _____
    _____

In analyzing the data from such an inventory, those pupils who may have indications of giftedness could possibly reveal one or more of the following characteristics:

1. Books secured for pleasure reading come from a number of different sources.
2. Several complete books have been read that involve various themes and subjects.
3. One or more hobbies are pursued on a regular basis.
4. Newspapers are read frequently by older pupils with special interest given to at least three or more sections.

The clues derived from studying the responses should be added to all other information gathered from both formal and informal devices. The total body of test data and responses should be of considerable help in completing the screening and nomination form which follows.

Screening and Nomination Form for Identifying Gifted and Talented Students

Name of Student _____ Teacher _____
Grade _____ Date _____ School _____

Place a check mark in the column which best describes the pupil in question.

	Yes	No	Sometimes
1. Displays a curious attitude toward a large number of subjects and shows an eagerness to learn as much as possible about several subjects.			
2. Exhibits the ability and desire to use a variety of plausible strategies for locating the answer to a precise problem or challenge.			
3. Recalls many kinds and types of detailed data for the purpose of forming meaningful main ideas, conclusions, and defensible generalizations.			
4. Shows a determined persistence when pursuing meaningful short and long-term goals and objectives.			
5. Demonstrates that he or she can delay a judgment on a controversial matter until all available facts both "pro" and "con" are studied.			
6. Senses different types of injustices which may exist in the immediate			

	Yes	No	Sometimes
environment as well as those that are national and worldwide.			
7. Displays a reluctance to accept or agree to statements or opinions which appear to be highly subjective in nature.			
8. Produces pieces of writing such as an original story or play that have identifiable plots and suitable endings.			
9. Makes a writing selection seem interesting and "lively" through the use of a large variety of words, phrases, and clauses which are placed in proper syntactical order.			
10. Demonstrates the ability to understand precise relationships that exist among a myriad of diverse and complex details.			
11. Perceives the role and nature of the social environment and how it affects the lives of different people.			
12. Understands the moods and intentions of both speakers and writers and constructs a proper response to these stimuli.			
13. Produces a large number of mental images and appropriate concepts in response to a challenging problem or question.			
14. Exhibits social skills which are appropriate for a given situation such as empathy, confidence, support, and understanding.			
15. Displays wide and diverse interests such as playing musical instruments, engaging in sports activities, and pursuing a variety of hobbies.			
16. Demonstrates an understanding of the meaning and use of a sizable number of words.			
17. Shows proficiency in the use of numerous fine and gross motor skills such as cutting, tracing lines, copying pictures, handling tools, and walking a balance beam.			

	Yes	No	Sometimes
18. Engages in meaningful constructive criticism of self and others in situations which are appropriate.			

It is expected that the referring teacher will be able to place a check mark in the "YES" column in the vast majority of the topics on the Screening and Nomination Form. Students who are thus nominated by this procedure should be further investigated with respect to the items mentioned previously such as individual I.Q. scores, data derived from numerous aptitude and achievement tests, and recommendations from other teachers. Particular attention should be given to the pattern of scores from various instruments rather than undue emphasis on the meaning of any one particular score.

RELATED PROCEDURES FOR IDENTIFICATION

In addition to the formal and informal procedures mentioned previously, an educator can engage in further research and study of various types to collect supplementary data for use in the proper identification of gifted and talented pupils. These procedures include a review of the past achievement record, nomination by fellow students, examination of projects completed by the nominee, study of the autobiography of the student, nomination by parents, and professional opinions of persons not associated with the child on a daily basis. A brief description of each of these procedures is provided in the remainder of this section.

1. *Review of Past Educational Record.* The truly gifted and talented pupil should establish an educational record of accomplishment which appears to be consistently much above average in virtually all areas of study. Past achievements can be estimated by studying such aspects as the kinds of grades received, data sheets from computer testing instruments, anecdotal records, and any written comments of achievements recorded by previous teachers.

Particular attention should be given to determine the level of academic achievement on standardized tests which has been attained. The truly gifted and talented child should demonstrate a consistently high level of achievement with regard to such items as grade placement scores, percentile rankings, and stanine marks. Notations indicating outstanding achievement such as honor roll designations and/or scholarship awards should be carefully studied.

School officials must attempt to analyze many other aspects of a pupil's past record besides classroom grades received. Unfortunately, a selected group of gifted pupils may, in fact, have records at the average or below average levels since they may find the school environment to be boring and frustrating due to a lack of proper challenge and stimulation on the part of teachers and the classroom setting in general. Letter grades assigned by classroom teachers tend to be subjective in nature and a pupil's potential level of achievement might possibly be higher than the grade(s) received. Previous grades should be considered as only one part of a learner's ability to accomplish goals and undertake various tasks.

2. *Peer Nominations.* Some authorities are of the belief that pupils in a particular grade or class may be excellent sources of information regarding the correct identification of the gifted and talented. The opinions may be derived through the use of a sociogram technique which suggests that the respondent supply the name of the child who best fits the descriptor item. Samples of such questions may be as follows:

   a. Of all of the pupils in this class, who do you think is first to answer the teacher's questions?
   _____

   b. Who is the best artist? _____

   c. Which person can explain things the best?
   _____

   d. Who do you think makes the highest score on achievement tests?
   _____

Because of the possibility that individual students may merely place the name of their best friend on the blank, the data obtained from such an instrument should be compared carefully with information secured from a number of different procedures or techniques.

3. *Projects or Products of the Learner.* Since artistic and musical talent is one of the identifying characteristics of many gifted and talented pupils, a careful examination of the art projects and other creative products may produce evidence relating to a learner's creativity. Viewing auditions relating to musical and/or dramatic activities may yield further data for screening. Carefully reading research papers, plays, and poems compiled by a pupil may also be helpful in the process of identification. Attendance at sports events may be an avenue for obtaining evidence relating to athletic abilities as well as gross and fine motor skills. Observa-

tion of learners while playing the role of an actor or actress in a school or community play may provide valuable evidence. Firsthand observations of pupils in a number of school and community functions is a valuable procedure for the identification and placement of gifted children in the school curriculum.

4. *Student Autobiographies and Interviews.* Much can be learned about the background and present interests of a pupil by reading autobiographies and completing interest inventories as well as conducting personal interviews to obtain data relating to hobbies, kinds of books read, and projects undertaken and constructed during previous years. An analysis of the information obtained from techniques and strategies of this nature serves to provide valuable, definitive concepts which could not be obtained in any other manner.

5. *Parent Nomination.* The correct identification of pupils for special placement in gifted curricula requires that personal accomplishments must be studied in *both* the school and home environments. A small number of gifted students may appear to be bored and frustrated in the school environment and display disruptive behavior and receive average to below average grades. Information obtained from parents can be helpful in learning about the total personality and ability level of the learner outside the school setting. Data relating to participation in community activities such as 4-H, Boy Scouts, and church groups can be helpful in understanding the actual and potential ability levels of the child.

6. *Opinions of Panel of Professionals.* In some instances school officials may wish to employ the use of a panel of community professionals to select pupils who should participate in specially designed instructional programs for the gifted and talented. Persons such as psychologists, social workers, business leaders, and curriculum specialists may be selected to serve on the panel. They could conduct interviews and review the papers, projects, and academic records of various students to make the final selection. These individuals may be especially objective since they probably have not had a long-standing personal relationship with any of the learners being considered.

SUMMARY

One of the most challenging aspects of the instructional program for the gifted and talented is that of identifying those students for special programs. There are numerous characteristics which should be considered such as creativity, leadership ability, level of motivation, and learning strategies. Formal and informal tests should be employed as well as other techniques such as peer nominations, examination of projects and products of the learner, parent nominations, and non-school professional panels.

REFERENCES

1. Labuda, Michael, "Gifted and Creative Pupils: Reasons for Concern," *Creative Reading for Gifted Learners*. Newark, International Reading Association, 1974, p. 2.
2. Buhler, Ernest O. and Eugene N. Guirl, "The More Able Student: Described and Rated," *Vocational Guidance Quarterly*, V. 8, N. 4 (Summer, 1960), pp. 217–221.
3. Marland, Sidney P., Jr. *Education of the Gifted and Talented*. Washington, D.C.: U.S. Department of Health, Education and Welfare, 1971, p. 2.
4. Mitchell, Patricia Bruce (Editor). *A Policymaker's Guide to Issues in Gifted and Talented Education*. Washington, D.C.: National Association of State Boards of Education, 1981, pp. 14–15.
5. Tuttle, Frederick B., Jr., and Laurence A. Becker. *Characteristics and Identification of Gifted and Talented Students* (Second Edition). Washington, D.C.: National Education Association, 1983, p. 13.
6. Guilford, J.B. *The Nature of Human Intelligence*. New York: McGraw-Hill Book Co., 1967.
7. Torrance, E. Paul. "Dare We Hope Again?" *Gifted Child Quarterly*, V. 22, No. 3 (Fall, 1978), pp. 292–312.

CHAPTER II

PLANNING AND IMPLEMENTING
SCHOOL PROGRAMS FOR THE GIFTED

After the important step of identifying gifted children has been accomplished by school authorities, the process of planning and implementing an appropriate school program for these learners must be undertaken. Such strategies must take into account a variety of factors including the objectives and/or principles of the curriculum, types of teachers needed as instructional leaders, and the means and methods for assessing the strengths and limitations of reading programs for the gifted.

In addition to these aspects, one must have a basic understanding of the historical development of educational programs for the gifted and talented in order to profit from the strengths and limitations of previous endeavors. The establishment of a well developed curriculum for these pupils is absolutely necessary if the full learning potential of each learner is to be realized. To provide the reader with the necessary background for constructing and implementing a proper program of instruction, the major topics mentioned in the previous sentences are discussed in this chapter. A summary and a body of references conclude the material.

HISTORICAL OVERVIEW OF EDUCATIONAL PROGRAMS
FOR GIFTED AND TALENTED STUDENTS

For many decades, educators have had an interest in identifying and educating those pupils who appeared to have talents and abilities much above what was considered average or normal for the general population. Those historians who emphasize the products of famous people frequently point to such persons as Albert Einstein, Thomas Edison, and Woodrow Wilson as being examples of individuals who were considered gifted. The genius of Einstein in producing the theory of relativity and Edison for developing the electric light are known to practically every

19

person who has studied the biographies of famous people. These individuals have had a significant impact on the lives of our citizens in the current generation.

It is interesting to note that these and other eminent leaders were plagued with other misconceptions and problems despite their qualities of giftedness. There is some evidence that Einstein was perhaps four years old before he could speak coherently and at least seven before he could read "according to grade level." As noted previously, Thomas Edison is remembered as one of the world's foremost scientists; however, one of his grammar school instructors reportedly told him he "was too stupid to learn anything." Walt Disney, the famous producer of children's print and electronic media projects, was once told by a certain newspaper editor that he was devoid of any creative ideas and subsequently dismissed him from his job at the newspaper office. Even though Wernher Von Braun was one of man's earliest scientists in space weapons, he was alleged to have made a failing grade in his secondary algebra class. Louisa May Alcott, the famous and creative writer, encountered numerous rejections from publishers for her early attempts. One editor informed her that he was of the opinion that she could never write anything which would have popular acceptance.

Goertzel and Goertzel[1] made a very prestigious and thorough study of the lives of 400 famous men and women who have made major contributions to society in such areas as science, government, and philosophy. As noted in their book, *Cradles Of Eminence,* they found that approximately one in four of these individuals was encumbered with a potentially disabling handicap despite their apparent giftedness in the area of their expertise.

A perusal of the biographies of these early gifted leaders leads one to draw several conclusions regarding their lives, occupations, and daily activities:

1. Gifted and talented adults are identified more often through the products of their daily endeavors rather than the subjective evaluation of one or more of their superiors.
2. Highly successful individuals are often the children of parents who have established significant records of accomplishment.
3. Persons who achieve greatness are often reared in home environments in which the parents foster a wide diversity of interests and have a sincere desire to help each child reach his or her maximum learning potential.
4. A significant number of prominent leaders attended private schools

where they received much individual attention and instruction for helping them learn as much as possible.

5. There is some evidence to suggest that highly gifted national and world leaders came from homes where other siblings appeared to be much more talented and creative than was true for the general population.

6. Contrary to current standards for the identification of the gifted, many famous individuals in the past two centuries tended to isolate themselves socially and intellectually from the citizenry in general and their peers in particular.

Early Diagnostic Procedures

The formal assessment of giftedness has a reasonably brief history. Mental testing of children for the purposes of identifying their relative potential for learning originated in about 1905 by Alfred Binet. In 1916, Lewis M. Terman published the first major revision of the *Stanford-Binet Intelligence Scale* and began using the term "intelligence quotient" to illustrate the general level of mental ability which a given individual may possess.[2] In 1937, Dr. Terman and Maud A. Merrill undertook a significant revision and renorming of the *Binet.* Further revisions and renorming took place in 1960 and 1972 and the test is still in use by clinical and school psychologists as an instrument for gaining valuable insights with regard to the *approximate* level of mental ability of clients.

The original Wechsler instrument, the *Wechsler-Bellevue Intelligence Scale* (1939), designed to assess the intelligence of adults, was revised in 1955 and renamed the *Wechsler Adult Intelligence Scale* (WAIS). The *Wechsler Intelligence Scale for Children* (WISC) was developed in 1949 and revised and restandardized in 1974.[3]

A significant objective of the use of intelligence testing in the early 1900's was for the placement of children who appeared to be mentally or emotionally deficient. The results of the instruments were *rarely* used for the purpose of special placement of pupils in public school classes or programs for the gifted and talented. Local and statewide regulations required that all children so placed had to be tested by qualified examiners. Level of intelligence as measured by individual instruments held a high priority with school officials. As noted in Chapter I, the *current* strategies for the placement of pupils in all kinds of special classes involve much more than the utilization of a single score from an intelligence test. Evaluation specialists realize that definite cautions should be exercised in the interpretation of the true meaning of such data. Such aspects as motivation and everyday classroom behavior should be studied carefully.

Evolution of Special Programs for the Gifted

A review of the programs and curriculum of some private schools in the middle and late 1800's reveals that provisions were made for special tutoring of exceptional children. Usually the pupils came from very advantaged homes whose parents were in the upper class of society. Special programs for children in public schools were very limited until the early 1900's when special advancement classes were established in such cities as San Francisco, Louisville, Winnetka, Columbus, and New York City.

From 1925–1959, Lewis Terman[4] undertook his famous longitudinal study of gifted children which provided important data for school officials relating to the construction of appropriate programs for gifted and talented children. The data revealed that a large number of the subjects could demonstrate superior reading ability previous to entering first grade. It became readily apparent that a curriculum for the especially bright and talented child was both urgent and necessary.

During the period of the Terman study, special programs for gifted children were developed at such locations as the University Elementary School at the University of California in Los Angeles. The New York City project was undertaken by Hollingsworth for the pupils who had I.Q.'s approaching 200.

The importance of intelligence level (especially mental age) as an aspect of the learning process was advanced by numerous educators and psychologists in the period from 1920–1930. Some leaders promoted the concept of establishing reading programs for very young children who were four years of age; however the results obtained from the famous Morphett-Washburne study[5] revealed that a mental age of at least 6.5 was necessary for young children to read successfully. Accordingly, many school officials delayed the start of some pupils in a reading program until they could demonstrate a mental age competency of 6.5. The results of several important studies undertaken shortly after the Morphett-Washburne investigation revealed that it *was not* necessary for a child to possess a minimum age of 6.5. Dr. Arthur Gates of Columbia University completed a very detailed study in 1937.[6] He found that when children were placed in small groups and provided with individualized instruction it was possible to teach children to read with a mental age as low as 4.5. He concluded that statements relating to a minimum mental age were basically meaningless.

CURRENT EXEMPLARY PROGRAMS FOR THE GIFTED

There are numerous educational programs in the United States at the present time which are truly exemplary in nature. Descriptions of selected programs follow along with the name of the person or agency to be contacted for further information.

I. *The Astor Program Model*

This special program is part of the New York City Schools curriculum and is designed especially for young pupils in the pre-kindergarten and kindergarten levels; however, some pupils at the basic primary and intermediate levels participate as well. The plan of study involves the participation of learners in study blocks which are structured to emphasize critical thinking skills and develop special interests. Additional attention is given to personal development which will lead to improved value structure and self-growth. (Director of Astor Program Model, Teachers College, Columbia University, Box 223, New York, NY 10027)

II. *Computeronics*

Emphasis is given in this special 35–40 hour course in computer training which will help to equip the learner to solve simple problems, undertake programming, and continually raise his or her level of general knowledge of the use of computer functions. Pupils can progress through the program at their own rate since specific units must be completed through the use of the mastery learning approach. The program is especially appealing to gifted and talented students since the program allows students to become proficient in the vocabulary of computer terms, learn how computers can be utilized in everyday life situations, and gain knowledge of how computers may be used in the future. (Program Director, Computeronics Program, Leon County Schools, 925-A Miccosukee Road, Tallahassee, Florida 32303)

III. *Individual Progress Program*

This curriculum project model was developed by the Seattle Public Schools for those pupils in Grades 2–5 who are achieving at the very highest levels in the basic core curriculum. Learners are carefully diagnosed when they enter the program and are grouped with other pupils with similar competency levels regardless of their current grade designation. Continual diagnosis is maintained to insure that children are properly assigned and achieving at their full potential. Besides the basic core curriculum, students in the programs are involved in a supplementary segment which concentrates on such topics as folk dance, media, art, and foreign languages.

The total program varies from a very structured to a flexible format depending upon the age of the learner. Community resources are used extensively to provide a wide variety of experiences. Additional class instruction is provided in the area of social and emotional avenues, interpersonal skills, awareness of the value of self-concept, and communication modes in everyday life. Six manuals are available for teachers who adopt the program. (Director, Individual Progress Program, Seattle Public Schools, 815 Fourth Avenue North, Seattle, Washington 98109)

IV. *Institute For Creative Education*

The Education Information and Resource Center in Sewell, New Jersey has developed a unique problem-solving curriculum of studies which can be used effectively with gifted learners. The major objective of the program is to help students develop the competencies necessary to respond appropriately to certain problems and questions with decisions which reflect originality, flexibility, and are well constructed. Pupils's skills can be improved to the point where they are proficient decision makers. The sequential series of lessons help teachers to guide alert pupils to understand complex situations which call for careful judgment and insightful thought processes. Teachers who utilize the program should avail themselves of specialized training which is available through the Institute. (Institute for Creative Education, Route 4, Box 209, Delsea Drive, Sewell, New Jersey 08080)

V. *Kids Interest Discovery Studies Kits*

This fascinating multimedia approach can be used with a large variety of pupils but is especially useful for gifted and talented learners. Kits are compiled which contain various media pieces such as models, study prints, tapes, and filmstrips which relate to a given topic of interest such as Astronomy, the Human Body, and Indians. Students are encouraged to conduct in-depth studies and produce a final product such as a tape, model, or photograph of some creative endeavor. Their projects may be added to an existing kit for further study by other pupils. Presentations by the learners to their parents and general public groups are encouraged. (Principal, Warder Elementary School, 7840 Carr Drive, Arvada, Colorado 80005)

VI. *Project Success Enrichment*

The P.S.E. program is especially constructed as an enrichment program for use with highly creative students in Grades 2–8. Pupils are grouped for two hours each week for enrichment classes of up to 15 students. One of the major curriculum areas for the program consists of various language arts topics such as enlarging vocabulary; reading award winning books; writing selected papers dealing with organization, editing and themes; and making oral reports relating to predetermined topics. The art curriculum involves such activities as drawing and painting with additional work in pottery projects consisting of numerous objects. The P.S.I. program can be integrated as a part of the regular classroom program or it can be utilized as a special "pullout" class to supplement the instructional daily class schedule of a given learner. (Director, Project Success Enrichment, 7249 Capitol Blvd. South, Tumwater, Washington 98501)

VII. *Sage Academic Achievement Program*

The Framingham, Massachusetts Public School System has developed a special instructional curriculum consisting of mini-units and independent study units to develop higher level critical, inductive, deductive, and creative thinking skills. The pupils in Grades 1–5 are also given special instruction in the processes of gathering data and information and organizing and integrating concepts in a functional and meaningful manner. An important segment of the program is independent study which provides the opportunity to selected learners to increase their levels of curiosity and knowledge in a number of subject areas. Data gathered from experimental studies involving Sage pupils and control groups indicated that the experimental (Sage) learners performed at a significantly higher level of thinking skills than did nonparticipants as measured by the *Ross Test of Higher Cognitive Processes* and the *Test of Cognitive Skills.* (Project SAGE, Barbieri School, Framingham Public Schools, Dudley Road, Framingham, Massachusetts 01701)

Further information regarding most of the previous programs can be secured by contacting the National Diffusion Network Division of the U.S. Office of Education. Each year this agency publishes a new edition of *Educational Programs That Work.* Copies of the publication are available from your state or regional NDN Facilitator who is usually associated with the state department of education. One can write directly to the national office which is in charge of administering the total body of programs. Their address is:

National Diffusion Network Division
U.S. Office of Education
1200 19th Street, N.W.
Room 714F
Washington, D.C. 20036
(Telephone 202-653-7006)

GUIDELINES FOR ESTABLISHING READING PROGRAMS FOR THE GIFTED

As noted in the previous section, there are numerous outstanding programs available for gifted children of all ages in the United States. Major emphases in the model curricula reveal a strong emphasis in the area of critical and creative thinking, science topics, and art projects. There are many aspects of the programs which can be utilized in the construction and development of effective reading programs for gifted and talented students at all chronological levels. The following is a list of these principles or guidelines along with a brief discussion of the importance of the item.

1. *The reading program for the gifted and talented pupil should be as individualized as possible.* Spache and Spache[7] are of the opinion that since these learners are pupils of high verbal ability, strong vocabularies and

quick learning aptitude, they can and do read more widely and deeply when the reading program is stimulating and challenging. For this reason they suggest the individualized approach to reading after the students have been introduced to reading through experience charts.

The individualized approach requires a careful evaluation of the pupil's *present* reading ability through the use of commercial and informal tests and observational techniques. The approximate independent, instructional, and frustration reading levels should be determined to help assure that the gifted learner is assigned suitable lessons in *instructional* level books and materials to prevent boredom and/or frustration.

A system of record keeping should be established to monitor each child's progress and provide reliable data for the purpose of ascertaining reading growth in the important skill areas such as word attack, comprehension, and vocabulary. Additional information could be obtained relative to titles of books read, reading interests, reviews of books, and personal viewpoints about hobbies and out-of-school activities.

2. *Provisions should be made for helping to insure that adequate amounts of inquiry reading are included in any program of instruction for the gifted.* Talented pupils should be given frequent opportunities during reading and the various core classes to investigate questions of inquiry which interest them. Each learner should be assigned a question and class discussions held regarding the techniques which may be employed for finding answers or responses to the question. These should include the use of specialized library resources, interviewing techniques, note taking, and report writing. After a problem or question has been researched, pupils should be provided an avenue or mechanism for sharing the data with class members. These aspects may include murals, skits, models, videotapes, and recordings. A formal class presentation may be made at which time the researcher provides a formal oral report of his/her research activities.

Swaby[8] suggests that a reading contract may be utilized as a motivational device for pupils who are undertaking inquiry projects. Included in such a contract may be assignments for skills development, comprehension activities, small group projects, and free reading activities. This strategy delineates the role and responsibilities of the learner for undertaking and completing a research project. The variety of requirements helps to insure a careful balance of skill development and reading interests.

3. *The reading curriculum for the gifted should provide many opportunities*

for extended reading of books and other print media which contain articles dealing with a wide range of topics and subjects. Since the able pupil is commonly interested in many subjects and problems, many resources must be available to meet the needs of the learners with respect to study and investigation. One of the most famous models for enrichment has been developed by Renzulli.[9] He believes that any curriculum which emphasizes a strategy of enrichment activities should provide a body of experience above and beyond the regular curriculum; show respect for students' interests; and take place at any time and place during the day when it is convenient. A variety of exploratory activities should be presented; the pupils should engage in group training sessions which involve brainstorming issues; and each learner should pursue an individual project for intensive research and investigation.

The extended reading program should make use of an extensive variety of literature which will tap the interests and abilities of all of the gifted students in a given room or school. The books should be carefully selected to include topics relating to science, social studies, drama, and all of the major areas in arts and science. One of the most extensive bibliographies which has been compiled for literature is by Mangieri and Isaacs.[10]

4. *The supplementary materials utilized with able students should contain a very limited amount of drill exercises.* Since these pupils learn at a much faster pace than average students, the discerning teacher should be careful to avoid "busywork" assignments just to keep the gifted child "busy and out of trouble." On some occasions one may find it necessary to use special practice assignments for individuals who demonstrate a particular need. Any homework required should be restricted to those lessons that have a high and intense interest and will result in a precise and definitive learning experience for the pupil. Examples of such activities may be research projects which entail the use of the public library for the collection of data and pertinent references.

5. *A careful analysis of each learner's strengths and limitations should be undertaken. The series of lessons should be directly related to the student's abilities and preferred learning modalities.* The evaluation program should include the administration and utilization of such commercial reading tests as the *California Reading Tests* (CTB); *Nelson-Denny Reading Test* (Riverside); and *Woodcock Reading Mastery Tests* (AGS). To develop data relating to preferred learning modalities one may wish to administer such instruments as *Test of Auditory Analysis Skills* (ATP); *Bruininks-*

Oseretsky Test of Motor Proficiency (AGS); *Bender Visual Motor Gestalt Test* (Psy. Corp); *Harris Tests of Lateral Dominance* (Psy. Corp); and *Wepman Auditory Discrimination Test* (WPS). Informal teacher-made tests and strategies such as the subjective reading inventory, cloze test, and stratified tests of spelling and word recognition may be used as well. Careful observation of the pupil engaged in everyday class situations may reveal important concepts and data regarding work habits, attitudes relating to challenging problems and situations, and degree of intensity with respect to assignment, research, and pleasure reading activities. Anecdotal information received from fellow instructors, classroom aids, and student teachers may also prove to be helpful.

6. *In some school environments it may be useful to establish special reading classes for those pupils who are especially gifted readers.* Many schools have utilized the *Joplin Plan*[11] as an organizational tool for grouping pupils in Grades 4–6. Students are carefully evaluated for placement in reading classes with learners who have similar abilities. For example, the sixth grade ability level class may contain four pupils from the fourth grade; six learners from Grade 5 and ten students from Grade 6. With this arrangement, gifted and talented students have the opportunity for engaging in challenging reading activities at their ability level without regard to their actual grade level.

7. *In order to provide gifted and talented pupils with appropriate experience in the classics, the use of the Junior Great Books Program may be advisable.* This program consists of a designated curriculum of interpretative reading and discussion for pupils who are enrolled in Grades 2–12. The major goals of the program are designed to aid the pupil to think reflectively and independently and listen and consider the thoughts and opinions of other persons. The pupils enrolled in the program are invited to read both traditional and modern stories as well as poetry and plays. The members of the Great Books Foundation in Chicago choose the selections for pupils at each learning level after examining and comparing the literature from lists and collections which have been compiled by local and national reading authorities, state reading consultants, and library association officers.

The authors of some of the books selected include Oscar Wilde, Rudyard Kipling, James Thurber, Hans Christian Andersen, Charles Dickens, Robert Browning, John Steinbeck, Robert Frost, Mark Twain, and William Saroyan. The total program exposes children to a wide selection of literature which helps them to engage in critical reading and culminates in the feeling of seeing books and classic print media as a source of enjoyment and enrichment.

8. *The use of a student contract may provide an invaluable source of enrichment for middle and upper elementary students.* The contract is a form or agreement which can be adopted for any content area; however, it is especially useful for the area of reading. The student and teacher are the major parties in the contract. The following are items which should be included as significant ingredients in curriculum contracts:

   a. Student's name, date, and grade
   b. Teacher's name and contract title
   c. Statements relating to behavior objectives for the agreement
   d. Methods or strategies to be employed to meet the completion of contract tasks
   e. Evaluation tools for determining if assignments have been met
   f. Places for indicating if conditions of the contract have been met
   g. Blank spaces for signatures of teacher and pupil

9. *If there is an atmosphere of congenial rapport in the classroom and school in general, especially talented readers may be selected and trained to be tutors for those classmates who need additional help in skills development.* Pupils chosen to be tutors should demonstrate that they have a caring attitude for others and can help the tutee realize that growth in reading skills is possible and practical. According to McNeil, Donaut, and Alkin[12] there are several principles which teachers should keep in mind when selecting and training tutors.

   a. Make tutors feel special and tell them that they have been carefully selected for the program.
   b. Inform them of the importance of constant reinforcement strategies which they should utilize with their "students." They should practice forming such statements as "Good try!" "Not quite, but almost" or "I had trouble with this, too."
   c. They should concentrate on a single reading skill for each lesson and be observant of the work habits, efforts, and skill achievement of the tutees.
   d. Tutors should practice saying and reading words with the classroom teacher before they are presented to the child receiving instruction.

10. *All homework assigned for gifted pupils should always be closely correlated to their assignments and never used as busywork.* Although the kind, amount, and frequency of assigned homework will depend on the reading level of the class or youngster, it is well to plan homework assignments that will let the child be successful in practicing a recently acquired

skill. Homework should always be a learning activity and never as a punishment.[13] The gifted and talented learner needs new and challenging assignments which will serve to enhance and build on earlier learning experiences. Any type of homework project should be for enrichment purposes.

In addition to the guidelines or principles stated previously, instructors need to remember several important general considerations when constructing programs and curricula. While most gifted children are excellent readers and engage in many reading activities, a few such learners have little interest in reading and may require additional instruction to develop and maintain grade level reading competencies. A small percent drop out of school or have little enthusiasm for entering higher education.

Since most gifted and talented students enjoy social situations, they should be placed in reading activities and assignments which allow them to express their ideas in many different topics and fields of study. Generally these pupils are most proficient in social leadership roles and tend to have very satisfactory levels of peer approval.

All children, including very able pupils, have a considerable range of individual differences. Because of this situation, it is not reasonable to try to group them in any type of strict homogeneous classroom setting with the goal of expecting them to perfect reading skills at the same levels as all other learners. Each student's set of interests, potential, and needs is unique, thus an instructional program which is highly individualized is needed and very necessary.

To gain their maximum potential, gifted learners must have many opportunities in classroom situations to develop their leadership abilities. In a reading group, the instructor may find it prudent to invite these children to chair the bulletin board committee, for example. The pupils may wish to display original illustrations or drawings of various scenes in a selection which has just been read.

In summary, in building a useful program of studies in reading for the able pupil, teachers need to design activities which are individualized and match the learner's potential and interests. Special groupings may be made for involving pupils in such programs as the Junior Great Books program and other curriculum patterns discussed in previous paragraphs.

TYPES OF TEACHERS NEEDED FOR THE GIFTED

There are many opinions and printed sets of standards which have been issued with regard to the characteristics and qualifications that should apply to those teachers who regularly instruct gifted children. Some states require specific course work and experiences before an endorsement or credential can be issued to a teacher applicant. A recent publication,[14] notes, for example, that the primary requirements for a teacher of the gifted in Connecticut include such aspects as a warmness and acceptance of these pupils; advanced graduate study relating to teaching assignment which increases his or her understanding of able students; and a willingness to seek further training.

A survey of officials in 149 school districts in 44 states which was conducted by McCormick and Swassing[15] produced data which revealed that in most of the school districts surveyed, no special criteria was developed to select teachers for extra classroom or combination programs that provide reading instruction for the gifted. The usual policy was simply to choose successful, experienced teachers who are interested in working with gifted students and then provide inservice training for them. A few schools hired only gifted specialists while others required that the instructor be certified in reading.

There appears to be a group of individuals who feel that the teacher of the gifted should have special training, especially if they are in a clinical setting. Some contend that a highly successful teacher who instructs average third and fourth grade children may not be the best person for working with gifted children.[16] In employing teachers of the gifted, special characteristics may be highly desirable such as the completion of special graduate courses and seminars dealing with classroom management techniques, providing for the individualizing of learning, and promoting creativity in teaching and learning. Additional knowledge and competencies should be obtained regarding the use of a variety of materials and equipment, structure and implement lessons dealing with various learning groups, and methods to employ in constructing a meaningful learning environment.

Ehrlich[17] believes that there is in fact no ideal teacher and no complex of traits which will identify a superior teacher of the gifted. She is of the belief that there are several characteristics which should be present regarding the teacher of the gifted and talented. These include intellectual superiority, empathy, acceptance, preparation, versatility, perceptiveness, flexibility, creativity, patience, and a sense of humor.

Since the teacher is perhaps the most important ingredient in any efficient program for the gifted, there appears to be a small number of very important characteristics which are vital if the individual is to function appropriately. One authority[18] believes that certain qualities are essential to the teacher of the gifted and talented: good academic record; keen interest in at least one academic or creative area; the ability to be flexible in such matters as time, materials, and instructional procedures; good sense of humor; and a person who is not easily intimidated.

Because the construction and development of large numbers of formal programs for the gifted is a fairly recent educational trend, the establishment of a nationwide consensus regarding the criteria needed for certification for teaching the gifted is conspicuously absent. In fact, the absence of special certification for gifted teachers in 34 states has already resulted in numerous "casualties" among their ranks. In some of these states, some trained professionals who have made a career commitment to education of the gifted are being replaced by teachers who are not only untrained in this area but, in some cases, do not want to work with gifted and talented children.[19]

Milgram[20] constructed a student rating scale entitled *Student Perception of Teachers* to measure instructor characteristics relating to cognitive, creative, and personal-social aspects. Though she utilized the instrument with both gifted and nongifted pupils in Israel, she is of the belief that the results could be generalized to educational situations in the United States. Her basic finding was that all children regardless of age, intelligence, and other factors believed that the level of intelligence of the teacher was the single most important characteristic of the instructor.

Some administrators appear to favor teachers for gifted programs who show characteristics of being gifted themselves such as high level of intelligence, creativity, and flexibility. These individuals show the ability to plan carefully for each pupil to help insure that maximum learning takes place. In many instances students perceive their instructors with these qualities as being highly successful.

To summarize, while some state educational authorities have designated courses and competencies for the certification of teachers of the gifted, many states allow any certified instructor to participate. The most ideal teacher of gifted children in the area of reading is one who has special certification as a reading specialist and has additional training in gifted child education. In addition, the individual should have an adequate level of intelligence and demonstrate abilities which illustrate flexibility and creativity.

ASSESSMENT OF STRENGTHS AND LIMITATIONS OF READING PROGRAMS FOR THE GIFTED

Reading programs for pupils of all ability levels should be evaluated on both a periodic and continuous basis to ascertain strengths and limitations of such important aspects as curriculum, materials used, and skill growth patterns of individual learners. The instructional strategies utilized with gifted and talented students need special attention.

There are two significant reasons for building a structured evaluation program. *First,* it is important because results of tests and anecdotal records provide a valuable benchmark for determining if instructional objectives and goals are being met. For example, if commercial achievement test data show a serious deficiency in certain areas of comprehension, teachers must restructure teaching plans to emphasize the skills which are limited.

Second, because a considerable amount of tax money is supplied for many gifted programs, the educators in charge of such endeavors *must* have current evaluative data to demonstrate that the levels of learning of the pupils is much higher than would be the case if no special provisions were made. Those in charge of the special program should respond to such questions as the following:[21]

   a. How have students benefited from this program?
   b. Are students operating more independently now than before?
   c. How well does the identification process work?
   d. How effective is the staff development component?

When undertaking a thorough program of assessment, it is important to remember several aspects. The next section contains a listing and explanation of five such principles.

Important Aspects of Reading Program Assessment

1. *It is significant to remember that the central purpose of assessment is to provide valuable data which will serve as the basis for program revision and improvement.* All lesson and unit plans for gifted pupils must be revised occasionally in light of the analysis of data obtained from both commercial and teacher-made tests. For example, it is imperative for the learners to utilize books and other print media which are at their *instructional reading level* (oral reading accuracy of 95 to 97 percent and silent reading comprehension of 75 to 89 percent). If any learner is currently reading in frustration or independent level materials, he/she should be given more appropriate teaching aids for use in daily assignments.

2. *The assessment of the value of the program and each student's progress in skill development should be approached from a broad perspective.* Assessment or evaluation most certainly consists of much more than the scores obtained from commercial and informal pencil and paper tests. Important information can also be secured through careful observation of a child's work habits and oral comments made in response to questions given during the reading class session. The investigation and analysis of test data and anecdotal entries on the cumulative folder may reveal valuable insights with regard to a child's past growth in reading skill development. Visits with parents during regularly scheduled parent-teacher conferences can result in the accumulation of concepts relating to a child's attitude toward his/her school experiences.

3. *When undertaking an evaluation program, the educator should analyze and study patterns of scores derived from various testing instruments.* Gifted and talented students may not score well on a given instrument due to test anxiety or a traumatic experience which occurred previous to the examination. In a few instances, highly able students may develop an attitude of boredom with regard to test taking and perform at a below average level. In making a definitive statement about a given learner's capabilities (or lack of), a careful analysis must be made of all evaluation data secured from numerous formal and informal measures of skills and abilities in reading.

4. *A carefully controlled balance of both commercial and informal tests should be used in any viable program of assessment.* Commercial and teacher-constructed tests have strengths and limitations. The major advantage of commercial standardized achievement tests is the norm-referenced segment which allows the teacher to make statistical comparisons of test

performance as applied to local and national groups of pupils and the student being tests. This aspect is important since a score such as the 90th percentile or the highest stanine is necessary for a learner to be placed in some gifted programs. Unfortunately, many commercial tests fail to evaluate the exact skill objectives promoted by the teacher.

Informal tests may be quite useful since they are designed to measure the level of a student's skill development with respect to those precise competencies emphasized by the teacher. They have the limitation of lack of comparison with other pupils on a regional or national basis.

Assessment should be undertaken to evaluate program objectives. Procedures should involve many different strategies and techniques of both formal and informal varieties. A careful balance of tests should be administered since various instruments have both strengths and limitations. (Chapter VI is concerned with a *detailed* description of an effective evaluation program.)

SUMMARY

Educational programs for gifted children have had a long and interesting history. In the early part of the present century numerous tests such as the *Binet* and *Wechsler scales* were used to measure intelligence. Formal programs for gifted children originated in the United States in the early 1900's. Currently, there are a number of exemplary programs for gifted pupils which are described in this chapter. There are a number of guidelines which should be followed in establishing and assessing reading programs for the gifted.

REFERENCES

1. Goertzel, V. and M. Goertzel. *Cradles of Eminence.* Boston, Little, Brown and Company, 1962.
2. Van Tassel-Baska, Joyce. *An Administrator's Guide to the Education of Gifted and Talented Children.* Washington, D.C., National Association of State Boards of Education, 1981, p. 9.
3. Slavia, John and James E. Ysseldyke. *Assessment in Special and Remedial Education.* Boston, Houghton Mifflin Company, 1978. pp. 234–235.
4. Terman, Lewis M. (Editor). *Genetic Studies of Genius.* Stanford, Stanford University Press, 1925–1959, Vols. 1–5.
5. Morphett, Mabel V. and Carleton Washburne. "When Should Children Begin to Read?" *Elementary School Journal,* V. 21 (March, 1931), pp. 496–503.

6. Gates, Arthur I. "The Necessary Mental Age for Beginning Reading," *Elementary School Journal,* 37 (March, 1937), pp. 498–508.

7. Spache, George D. and Evelyn B. Spache. *Reading in the Elementary School* (Fifth Edition). Boston, Allyn and Bacon, Inc., 1986, p. 323.

8. Swaby, Barbara E. R. *Teaching and Learning Reading, A Pragmatic Approach.* Boston, Little, Brown and Company, 1984, p. 267.

9. Renzulli, Joseph S. "The Enrichment Triad Model: A Guide for Developing Defensible Programs for the Gifted and Talented," *Gifted Child Quarterly,* V. 20 (Winter, 1976), p. 3.

10. Mangieri, John N. and Carolyn W. Issacs. "Recreational Reading for Gifted Children," *Roeper Review,* V. 5, N. 3 (February, 1983), pp. 11–14.

11. Cushenbery, Donald C. "The Joplin Plan and Cross Grade Grouping," *Organizing For Individual Differences.* Newark, Delaware, International Reading Association, 1967, pp. 33–46.

12. McNeil, John D., Lizbeth Donaut, and Marvin C. Alkin. *How to Teach Reading Successfully.* Boston, Little, Brown and Company, 1980, pp. 302–303.

13. Ibid, p. 296.

14. Mitchell, Patricia Bruce (Editor). *A Policymaker's Guide to Issues in Gifted and Talented Education.* Washington, D.C., National Association of State Boards of Education, 1981, p. 40.

15. McCormick, Sandra and Raymond H. Swassing. "Reading Instruction For The Gifted: A Survey of Programs," *Journal for the Education of the Gifted,* V. 5, N. 1 (Winter, 1982), pp. 34–43.

16. Fox, Lynn H., Linda Brody, and Dianne Tobin (Editors). *Learning-Disabled/Gifted Children Identification and Programming.* Baltimore, University Park Press, 1983, p. 263.

17. Ehrlich, Virginia Z. *Gifted Children, A Guide for Parents and Teachers.* Englewood Cliffs, Prentice-Hall, Inc., 1982, pp. 119–122.

18. Van Tassel-Baska, Joyce. *op. cit.,* p. 30.

19. Renzulli, Joseph S. "Are Teachers of the Gifted Specialists? A Landmark Decision of Employment Practices in Special Education for the Gifted," *Gifted Child Quarterly,* V. 29, N. 1 (Winter, 1985), p. 24.

20. Milgram, R. M. "Perception of Teacher Behavior in Gifted and Nongifted Children," *Journal of Educational Psychology,* V. 71, N. 1 (February, 1979), pp. 125, 128.

21. Van Tassel-Baska, *op. cit.,* p. 31.

CHAPTER III

MEETING THE INSTRUCTIONAL NEEDS OF GIFTED PRIMARY CHILDREN

The process of reading skill development requires the inclusion of a carefully chosen list of competencies which helps to insure that the young learner develops into a competent, literate member of society. The nature of the basic requirements should have the common elements of word analysis, comprehension, and vocabulary proficiencies. For gifted and talented pupils an expanded statement of auxiliary goals should be developed to help these children construct a maximum level of learning ability.

Special provisions must be undertaken to provide for the important aspects of readiness and extended reading since a few highly gifted pupils may enter school with intermediate grade level reading ability. Obviously, curriculum alternatives must be made to account for this fact. The ability of the teacher to provide an individualized program for truly gifted young readers is imperative if boredom and disenchantment are to be eliminated.

The major purpose of this important chapter is to provide a description of a suitable reading program for young children in general and gifted pupils in particular. The major aspects of the topic include a discussion of the components of a suitable readiness curriculum; factors related to readiness; important methods and procedures for evaluating the primary child's present level of reading skill development; reading instructional strategies for the gifted primary child; and effective parent-teacher relationships for aiding the young gifted reader.

COMPONENTS OF A SUITABLE READINESS CURRICULUM

During the past several decades numerous educators and psychologists have emphasized the importance of building appropriate physical, mental, and educational skills as a basis for becoming an effective and competent reader at all grade and learning levels in the school system.

Psychologists such as G. Stanley Hall and Arnold Gessel undertook studies which resulted in the widely accepted belief that as children grew and matured they evolved through various, well-defined levels of development in the physical and mental realms. They discovered that no two children have the same degree of behavioral maturity and thus must be carefully evaluated to help determine if they are ready to undertake and master certain educational tasks, especially reading skills.

By the early 1920's, several nationally known tests had been developed for the evaluation of general achievement and intelligence. The *Binet* and *Wechsler Scales* for assessing intelligence and general behavioral characteristics were in use by many educational and psychological specialists. The 1916 *Binet Scale* attempted to provide standards of intellectual performance for average American-born children from ages three to young adulthood which was assumed, on the basis of available information for purposes of the scale, to be age 16. Tests were arranged in order of difficulty by age levels. The intellectual ability of an individual, determined by his/her performance on the scale, was judged by comparison with the standards of performance for normal children of different ages.[1]

Through the use of these and other instruments in controlled studies, various investigators concluded in the early 1930's that a minimum mental age of 6.5 was necessary for a child to enjoy reading success in the first grade. The term "mental age" was commonly utilized as a standard by which a specialist could determine the magnitude or degree of proficiency of mental functioning. As noted earlier, the famous Morphett-Washburne study[2] of 1931 conducted in Winnetka, Illinois resulted in the widely accepted belief that no formal reading instruction should take place for any child unless he or she could demonstrate a mental age of 6.5 as measured by a reputable intelligence test. According to Swaby[3], the initial view of readiness accepted from 1900 to approximately the mid-1930's focused on physical and mental maturation and thus the total responsibility for readiness was placed on the child. If the child did not have a sufficient level of maturation when entering first grade, formal reading instruction was delayed until the child matured.

Since 1960, educators have concluded that a number of guiding principles should be kept in mind when constructing readiness activities and programs for young children. Some of these are:

1. **There are many factors involved in determining if adequate readiness for reading has been established. These include physical, emotional, educational, mental, and environmental aspects.**

2. Developing an appropriate level of readiness for reading is not a product of an accumulation of time but rather the impact of experiences offered to the young child.
3. The teacher's methods of teaching and his or her reward system has a significant relationship to the degree of success a learner may have in achieving reading success.
4. Readiness for learning of all kinds is necessary with regard to all content fields of study.
5. There are many different formal and informal methods and strategies for assessing readiness to read and data collected from *all* of these instruments and strategies should be considered when making decisions relating to total reading readiness.
6. Since various kinds of teaching require unique readiness requirements, the methods utilized for determining readiness should be especially chosen to assess definitive characteristics.
7. A careful study of a child's total readiness profile should be undertaken to determine the methods of instruction which would be most useful.
8. Readiness skills are linked to a child's previous background of experience and thus a variety of informal strategies must be utilized to assess this important aspect.

FACTORS RELATED TO READINESS

There are many factors that are directly related to a young child's readiness to read. Before discussing these aspects one must realize that readiness for reading is a relative matter depending greatly on what is to be learned and how it is to be represented. Reading can be defined in a number of ways, thus making various learning tasks more or less appropriate depending on what is valued.[4] The term "reading readiness" may be applied to a condition or stage of education growth which a child has reached which allows him or her to read without attendant discomfort of a psychological or physical nature. The beginning of the growth of reading readiness occurs at birth and continues throughout one's lifetime until death. *Beginning* readiness is related to those skills and abilities which are developed previous to entering school at the kindergarten and/or first grade level. *Specific* readiness is important at all age levels. The material in this chapter is concerned primarily with the *beginning* stage.

Parents and teachers have a common responsibility for building certain attributes of readiness. These include such aspects as mental abilities, background of experience, social and language development, and physical characteristics. Each of these factors (as well as others) is discussed with respect to its importance in the sections which follow.

Mental Abilities

For many years the aspect of the importance of intelligence as reflected by mental age and verbal and nonverbal abilities has been considered a significant factor with regard to a child's ability to read effectively. (As noted earlier, the data derived from the Morphett-Washburne study of 1931 suggested that a child needed to demonstrate a minimum mental age of 6.5 to be a successful reader.) In 1953, Sister Mary Nila's in-depth study[5] revealed the conclusion that the factors related to reading readiness in order of importance were auditory discrimination, range of information, and mental age. The Gates study discussed in Chapter 2 disputed the importance of a minimum mental age and concluded that the aspect of the method of instruction used was more vital than the level of intelligence of the learner.

One of the most recent studies involved with the importance of intelligence was conducted by Stanovich, Cunningham, and Feeman in 1984.[6] They concluded that while general intelligence had some relationship to reading ability there were other qualities such as verbal comprehension abilities, phonological knowledge, and reading speed which should be studied carefully before determining a child's ability to read effectively.

Aukerman and Aukerman[7] suggest that while a mental age of about six years is required for formal reading, the exact level which is necessary is dependent on the learning environment in which a child is placed. A child in a small clinic or laboratory situation could function with a lower mental age than when he or she is in a classroom situation. A careful evaluation of a young learner's level of mental development can be assessed through the use of both formal and informal means.

There are several *group* intelligence tests that measure a variety of skills which are closely related to success in reading. These give an indication relative to such aspects as a child's background of understanding, skill in following directions, vocabulary ability, understanding of common analogies, and basic reasoning. Since little or no actual reading is demanded, the use of such tests as the following may be advantageous: *SRA Primary Mental Abilities Test* (S.R.A.); *Otis-Lennon School Ability Test* (Psychological Corporation); and the *California Test of Mental Maturity* (California Test Bureau). *Individual* intelligence tests yield data and pertinent information relative to a learner's mental potential. Two of the most prominent instruments of this type are the *Revised Standford-Binet Intelligence Scale* (Riverside) and the *Wechsler Preschool and Primary Scale of Intelligence* (Psychological Corporation). These two instruments require administration by a trainer examiner who is properly licensed. Some reading specialists and other school officials often utilize additional intelligence tests to gain an estimate of intellectual ability. Two such instruments are the *Slosson Intelligence Test* (Slosson) and the *Peabody Picture Vocabulary Test* (American Guidance).

In evaluating the composite level of general intelligence, the results of both commercial and informal tests should be utilized along with the impressions received from careful observation and discussion with the pupils. A study of these data will help to provide significant information relating to the nature and level of giftedness which may be evident with respect to a particular pupil.

Background of Experience

The experiences which a young child has encountered have a significant relationship to having a proper level of knowledge and skill for undertaking formal reading assignments. Those children whose parents are suitable role models are likely to come to school with the ability to express a broad speaking and writing vocabulary and possess concomitant levels of understanding with respect to words that are spoken and seen in print. Hopefully, they have seen their parents and siblings reading books and other printed material with joy, pleasure and anticipation. Books and magazines which are readily available in the home environment lead the child to want to interpret the meaning of pictures and letters.

Unfortunately, a significant segment of kindergarten and first grade children are not exposed to the favorable conditions just described. Perhaps they are children of parents who, because of certain economic and sociological reasons, cannot provide for reading materials and quality time periods when reading activities may take place. Some instructors conclude that a child who is reared in an economically deprived home environment is automatically educationally disadvantaged. Harris and Sipay[8] believe that it is a mistake to draw this conclusion and contend that many children who are normal in intelligence come to school from homes that are quite lacking in intellectual stimulation.

Language skills which entail both oral and written vocabulary are closely related to a child's home environment. Children need to hear proper speech in a variety of situations. The printed word only has meaning when the reader has had some experiences which produce an understanding of what the word means. In an ideal home environment the child has had some experiences which produce an understanding of what the word means. Hopefully, the child has had a chance to hear parents speak with a broad range of words. With this type of situation, he or she tends to imitate the language heard and uses sentences which contain a variety of words and are in correct syntactical patterns. Opportunities for further oral and written vocabulary occur when the young child visits a multitude of community sites such as the zoo, local stores, and museums. At the zoo, for example, they grasp the understanding of the word "elephant" when they see the huge animal foraging for pieces of alfalfa bales which have been placed in his pen by the zoo keeper. At the museum, the word "fossil" becomes meaningful when the young boy or girl observes the hardened remains of a prehistoric plant such as a fern or a piece of coal or rock. Verbal explanations of such an exhibit by a museum official could lead the child to learn and use many additional new words such as "remains," "traces," and "formed."

The home environment has a significant influence on the development of appropriate work and study habits of the learner. In the school setting, the teacher has the expectation that the pupil understands the necessity for taking turns, sharing materials, and respecting the rights of others. Unless these habits have been developed, he or she will encounter significant difficulties in relating to classmates with regard to sharing books, word cards, and other materials. Students need to understand that they are in a social environment while a member of the reading class or group and regardless of learning level achieved, they must expect to conform to a certain body of classroom behavior standards.

A child's background of experience can be assessed in a formal sense through the use of some types of reading readiness and intelligence tests. During the administration phase the following items may be tested:

1. *Perceiving relationships* (You have fingers on your hands and _____ on your feet.)
2. *Breadth of Knowledge* (Where does wood come from?)
3. *Opposites* (What is the opposite color of black?)

4. *Sequence of events* (Show child five different aspects of a simple comic strip. Place them in scrambled order on a table and ask him/her to put them in right order.)

On all of the previous items, the very gifted and able child should be able to answer all of the items with little or no hesitation. Ekwall[9] found that the gifted young children he studied came from homes where abundant opportunities were given for varied experiences and total exploration of the environment. Language experiences and sensorimotor activities were rich and were combined with numerous activities for intellectual stimulation. Various other studies appear to provide considerable evidence that those children who have a rich and varied background in language development are much more likely to succeed in beginning reading tasks than those who have been severely disadvantaged in this regard.

Those pupils (including the gifted) who have a limited background of experience obviously need to be exposed to a large number of school experiences to enhance this aspect of the teaching-learning process. To improve oral and written skills may dictate the use of the language experience approach. In this method the child's own oral language serves as the basis for stories compiled on a piece of paper by the teacher. Suggested additions to the selections by various pupils and the teacher can serve to greatly accentuate a young reader's total store of oral and written vocabulary.

In summary, the young gifted child needs a broad latitude of experiences which will correlate with the numerous new words and phrases which he or she constantly encounters. Special attention should be given to such aspects as bulletin boards, displays, and exposure to new books and magazines that include a sizable amount of new words and concepts.

Physical Aspects

There are many significant factors in the physical realm which have a direct bearing on a child's readiness to read. These include motor development, auditory acuity and discrimination, and visual discrimination and acuity. A careful assessment of the present status of each of these aspects allows the teacher to cooperate with the parents in building each component for maximum growth in beginning reading activities.

Small and large motor development begins to occur at birth and those children who are otherwise healthy encounter numerous opportunities for walking, running, and jumping. Planned playground activities in the school setting add immeasurably to a child's level of motor skills. Fine motor activities can be enhanced considerably by coordinated hand-writing activities as well as by craft projects which may correlate with language arts activities. Farr and Roser[10] contend however, that the relationship of motor development to readiness for reading is unclear. Behaviorally, children who demonstrate readiness can listen to a story read to them, do simple copy work, and turn a page.

Auditory acuity is vital to reading success since the ability to hear words distinctly and apply auditory sounds to visual symbols is the key to understanding words. The level of acuity can be checked by the school nurse to gain relative data concerning any possible decibel loss. Teachers should be alert to any outward signs displayed by the learner such as the cupping of hands by the ears or repeated requests to have oral announcements and directions repeated. Oral reading undertaken by the child can yield important empirical evidence relating to whether or not the pupil is saying the words the way they were heard.

The English language contains a massive amount of words which sound very similar, e.g., may-nay; bolt-boll; mit-met; car-par, etc. As noted earlier, Sister Nila's well documented study indicated that the ability to discriminate between and among sounds is the single most important factor related to beginning reading. There is some evidence to suggest that those students who are engaged in intensive phonics programs develop higher levels of skills in discrimination abilities since they are attuned to the individual sounds which various letter and letter combinations make in special settings. A sound phonics training background would seem to be especially valuable for the more able child as he or she engages in the pronunciation of longer and more difficult words.

Since the first part of the reading act is concerned with the establishment of a visual image of the word or symbol on a page or signboard, the factor of visual acuity or the degree of sharpness of vision is extremely important. Many young children have far-point and near-point vision problems. Teachers who detect signs of visual problems such as swollen and discharging eyes, reddened pupils, headaches, and/or dizziness difficulties should refer the learner to the school nurse for screening by such instruments as the *Massachusetts Vision Test; Keystone Visual Survey Tests; Sight Screener;* or the *Titmus School Vision Tester.* If pronounced difficulties are revealed by tests, the parents of the learner should be advised to consult with a seeing specialist such as an optometrist or opthamologist. Professional examinations by these specialists may reveal the probable cause of any visual acuity difficulty. Appropriate remedial procedures may include the prescribing of eyeglasses or contact lens as well as eye drops for infectious and innerocular pressure.

Even though the young child may exhibit appropriate visual acuity, he or she may encounter visual discrimination problems. In these cases a number of procedures and strategies may be employed such as practice book exercises provided by basal reader publishers and other companies which are noted in the appendices section of this volume. In recent years special instructional programs for improving a pupil's skill level in such areas as figure-ground perception, constancy of perception, perception of position in space, and perception of spatial relationships have been constructed. One such program was constructed by Marianne Frostig and David Horne which was entitled *The Frostig Program for the Development of Visual Perception* and published by Follett. Several research studies have been conducted regarding the value of the Frostig program and the results have been mixed. One major problem suggested by Cohen[11] and Wingert[12] is that the structured activity work on the exercises failed to transfer into definitive reading growth. There are several types of teaching materials listed in the appendices section which may be useful for helping a child improve visual skills.

General physical health relating to such aspects as proper nutrition and appropriate growth development are important for proper functioning of the learner in a reading environment. The absence of chronic health problems allows the pupil to attend classes on a regular basis and learn basic reading skills when they are presented in a sequential manner by the instructor.

Emotional Health

In order to build a successful background for formal reading, it is necessary for pupils to develop certain attitudes. Harris and Smith[13] note that children must have a healthy self-concept that permits them to persist in the face of adversity. This aspect allows them to take turns, respect the rights of others, and pursue a learning task until it is completed. Young children entering kindergarten or first grade exhibit a wide range of emotional structures. Some display a feeling of cheerfulness and stability while others show immature tendencies and appear babyish by engaging in temper tantrums and demonstrating anti-social behavior. The latter children may resent supervision by the teacher and resist cooperation with the total class when sharing materials.

The success that a pupil may achieve in reading skill development has a significant correlation to his or her ability to socialize in the school setting. Before arrival at school, many learners have been the center of attention in the family environment and little experience has been gained in situations which require a close working relationship with peers. The realization that being a member of a cooperative group is a prerequisite for reading success causes some trepidation for socially deficient children. Later in this chapter an informal observation instrument is included which notes some of the questions and concerns which should be assessed in the social and emotional realms.

Cultural Considerations

The cultural nature of a learner's home and immediate environment has a high degree of relationship and importance to the general level of reading readiness which may be in evidence. Pupils who are raised in an environment, for example, which is economically deprived are typically at a much greater disadvantage with regard to reading and language development than those pupils who are privileged to be in advantaged situations. Ramsey[14] discovered in his study that the economic situation of a school district also has a close relationship to the level and nature of reading achievement of the pupils. Those schools in Kentucky in the upper quarter of achievement also allocated much greater amounts of money for instructional materials than did those schools listed in the lower three quarters of achievement.

The social class to which a child belongs also has a significant bearing on his or her level of readiness for reading. Some sociologists are of the belief that many pupils who come from lower class environments often have less than average levels of mental development, lack stimulation for maximum reading development, and suffer from an absence of parental role models which are necessary for proper attitudes regarding reading and learning. Other cultural and environmental aspects that may have a significant impact on reading readiness are the educational level of the parents; family size; and location of the primary residence of the family. Because of the emphasis given by many school authorities for constructing academic programs for those in the middle social and economic class, the pupils who come to school from lower class situations find that they are at a disadvantage in attempting to cope with the demands of the school in general and some teachers in particular.

Sex Differences

Several studies have been conducted to determine if either girls or boys seem to be more ready to read at an early age. Generally, girls mature at a faster pace than boys and thus have a tendency to begin formal reading sooner than boys. However, Ralph Preston's[15] famous study in 1979 of a large number of primary children in Germany resulted in the conclusion that there was little, if any, difference in reading skill development when comparing boys and girls. An implication of the study may be derived to suggest that a child's immediate school and home environment may have a much more significant influence on reading growth than the factor of sex differences.

METHODS AND PROCEDURES FOR EVALUATING THE PRIMARY CHILD'S PRESENT LEVEL OF READING SKILL DEVELOPMENT

While one of the first and most primary responsibilities of school personnel is that of identifying gifted children, the intensive analysis of each young child's reading strengths and limitations is vital and necessary. The assessment procedures should be designed to measure a learner's present skill abilities in the basic competency areas of reading: word attack; comprehension; vocabulary; reading readiness; and oral reading. In conducting such an evaluation, one may utilize commercial reading readiness and reading achievement tests, informal oral reading tests, and subjective reading inventory examinations which yield valuable information relating to the pupil's independent, instructional, and frustration reading levels. The total body of data should be of immeasureable help in determining the degree and kind of giftedness which a given learner exhibits in the area of reading development.

Particular attention should be given to the area of comprehension with special emphasis given to how well the gifted child is able to deal with such aspects as the following:

a. Main idea of a selection which is read silently or orally.
b. Value judgments derived from careful reasoning processes.
c. Inference selected from the context of a selection.
d. Awareness of the basic plot structure.

Competency Chart

A competency chart which deals with the major skills and abilities expected in reading can be constructed. At the top of the sheet one can list desired skills and abilities with the names of the students listed in a vertical manner on the left side of the page. The following is a sample chart which may be utilized.

READING SKILLS COMPETENCY CHART FOR GIFTED STUDENTS

Names	Skills and Abilities			
	Pronunciation of Words	Oral Reading	Critical Reading	Listening
1. Elizabeth	Excellent at all levels	Usually accurate	Needs work on propaganda techniques	Attends to all oral comments very satisfactorily
2. Harold	Very good except in structural analysis	Needs help in reading multisyllabic words	Difficulty with making judgments	Understands and follows oral directions
3. Hardwick	Shows skill in pronouncing most words	Excellent ability in enunciation and expression	Knows how to differentiate fact from opinion	Tends to engage in passive listening
4. Becky	Clear in speaking	Projects feeling and confidence	Makes simple inferences	Displays ability to be active listener

The competency chart indicates several pronounced strengths and limitations with regard to the acquired reading skills of each pupil. The following assumptions may be made about each learner.

1. *Elizabeth* pronounces words correctly and exhibits satisfactory oral reading skills, but needs further work in critical reading, especially with regard to propaganda techniques.
2. *Harold* is a good listener but has some deficiencies with regard to word attack and oral reading.
3. *Hardwick* displays excellent overall reading skill development but needs to become an active listener.
4. *Becky* shows a high level of proficiency in all of the major areas of reading proficiency.

Reading Readiness Qualifications Evaluation

In addition to utilizing the previous chart, the evaluation of a young child's readiness to pursue formal reading skill lessons may be estimated by writing "yes" or "no" before the following statements. (A young learner who has *gifted* tendencies should demonstrate at least 90 percent "yes" responses for each of the following sections.)

I. *Physical Qualifications*

_____ 1. Shows that bodily movements are well coordinated.

_____ 2. Demonstrates ability to distinguish visually the likenesses and differences among and between figures, words, objects.

_____ 3. Hears likenesses and differences between and among different types of words and phrases.

_____ 4. Pronounces words with no evidence of "baby talk" or stuttering.

II. *Social, Mental, and Emotional Adjustment*

_____ 1. Seems happy, alert, and relaxed in schoolroom situations and displays a willingness to interact with peers.

_____ 2. Follows directions and has a long attention span.

_____ 3. Relates events in order of story which has been read to him or her.

III. *Background of Interests and Attitudes*

_____ 1. Shows an interest in books and reading in general.

_____ 2. Shares books with peers and the teacher during formal and informal class situations.

_____ 3. Appears to like stories to be read to him or her.
_____ 4. Displays an immediate interest in new books which have been placed in the room and/or school library.

IV. *Language Development*

_____ 1. Demonstrates the ability to speak and write a large number of words which are common to the learning level of the pupil.
_____ 2. Speaks in full sentence patterns and uses a large variety of descriptive words to illustrate topics and ideas being discussed.
_____ 3. Shows evidence of a high degree of general verbal facility.

Typically, the young gifted pupil displays practically all of the previous tendencies and projects the general attitude that the total act of reading is pleasurable, profitable, and exciting. It is important for the teacher to undertake the various instructional strategies described in the next major section with these children, otherwise boredom can develop along with possible behavior problems.

Functional Reading Appraisal

During the school day a primary child will have a need to make use of a number of books and resources in addition to the basal reader. Instructors must have a clear understanding of the level of proficiency which a young learner can demonstrate when utilizing a variety of volumes such as the classroom dictionary, social studies text, and the weekly paper (such as the *Weekly Reader*). A simple exercise such as the following may be employed as a diagnostic tool for ascertaining the degree to which a child has mastered the correct use of the adopted science book.

1. On what page does Chapter 2 begin? _____
2. Write the name of the chapter that tells about the weather. _____
3. Write the number of the page where the index begins. _____
4. Look on Page 29. How tall is the elephant which is shown in the picture? _____
5. Read the table of contents. Does this book tell about jungle animals? Yes or no.

Teacher Observation

The observation of pupil behavior in reading situations provides the teacher with very important data and general information which cannot be obtained by the use of any other technique or strategy. The degree of giftedness displayed by a primary child may be judged to a degree by attending to aspects such as the following:

a. Signs of eagerness and enthusiasm with regard to the total activity of reading.
b. Indication of anticipation for a trip to the library for free reading and the examination of new books.
c. Participation in discussions and group projects which require diversity in reading.
d. Engagement in wide reading for genuine pleasure and enjoyment.
e. Demonstration of proficiency in locating information and selecting materials.
f. Projection of genuine desire to read through the sharing of books and stories during conferences and "show-an'tell" periods.

Through the systematic use of data gathered during careful observations, the instructor comes to know much about each learner's competencies, interests, tastes, and attitudes. To supplement these data, carefully planned conferences may be undertaken to fill in the gaps with information not observed on earlier occasions. The impressions gained during the personal conferences serve as a basis for planning precise instructional reading programs that meet the individual needs of the gifted and talented child who may be performing at an achievement level two or three levels above the grade where the pupil is enrolled. The combined information derived from commercial tests, teacher-made instruments, and observational strategies may serve as the basis for important decisions such as accelerated placement, membership in enrichment groups, and special gifted programs which have been established by local and state educational authorities.

Use of Anecdotal and Cumulative Records

It is difficult for any teacher to depend entirely upon memory for outlining the strengths of many very able learners in a primary school situation. Anecdotal records are valuable since they provide the basis for forming attitudes and opinions relating to such important matters as a child's behavior pattern, reactions to particular situations, and general work habits. For example, one may find statements such as the following included on the record sheets of able second grade pupils: "Rachel read *The Adventures of Tom Sawyer* and wanted to share it with her peers," "Matthew read a section of a *World Book* article and pronounced all of the multisyllabic words with ease," "Melissa read an article from last night's newspaper and shared it with the class with an accompanying illustration."

The cumulative record folder containing information about teacher observations, reports of conferences with parents, results of mental and achievement test results, physical examination reports, and other data can be extremely important in determining the degree and kind of giftedness displayed by a child. The vital concept to keep in mind is that a single test score, data from competency charts, observational data, and impressions gained from anecdotal and cumulative records must be carefully integrated and considered in a global sense before making final educational decisions.

Chapter VI of this volume contains valuable comprehensive information relating to the total process of evaluation of the reading skills of gifted and talented learners.

READING INSTRUCTIONAL STRATEGIES FOR THE GIFTED PRIMARY CHILD

The usual scope and sequence chart for any organized basal reading program typically lists a large number of competencies, goals, and objectives in the major skill areas of word attack, comprehension, and resource reading. Many of the teacher's guides contain specific suggestions for instructional strategies for able children. The descriptions of the plans which follow are samples of the activities which may be utilized.

The Language Experience Approach

As noted by Rubin[16], the language experience approach utilizes the experiences of children, is nonstructured, based on the inventiveness of both teacher and students, and brings together all of the language arts. The basic ingredient in the method is the recording of an experience (or a body of activities) which has been encountered by a child. The story or episode is written with the pupils supplying the basic elements of the semantic structure. The young gifted child typically demonstrates his/her proficiency in supplying interesting and colorful modifiers for the subject, predicate, and object segments of sentences. The activity provides unlimited opportunities for these children to explore complex concepts and at the same time enlarge sight word vocabulary, improve phonic and structural analysis proficiency, and increase generally all phases of comprehension including literal meaning, interpretative ideas, critical concepts, and creative feelings. The following is a selection which was dictated by a group of able third grade pupils. Within the selection one can easily notice the level of difficulty of concepts and vocabulary structure which is possessed by the learners.

The Fire in the Art Room

Yesterday afternoon several boys and girls noticed some dark smoke coming from the art room. Mary Louise raced excitedly to the principal's office to report the event. Mrs. Everworth, our efficient secretary, quickly communicated with the fire department on Harney Street and in no time at all the firefighters came to our building. They found an enormous stack of multi-colored construction paper on fire. The immediate burst of water from the enlarged fire hoses put the fire out in a hurry. We are grateful for the competent work of our firefighters.

Through this exercise, the pupils were exposed to an effective means for sight word enlargement and vocabulary meaning. For some children, the following words were added to their reading, speaking, and writing vocabularies: *excitedly, efficient, communicated, enormous, multi-colored, immediate, grateful,* and *competent.* The teacher may re-read the selection and ask the following questions for the purpose of refining various word attack and comprehension skills.

1. Can you find the word *"efficient"*? Louise, would you go to the chart and point to the word?
2. Who can find a word in our story which means the same as large or big?
3. How many words can you find which have more than one syllable? Let's all write them on a piece of paper and see who has the longest list.
4. Look at the story again. See if you can find a word which rhymes with "bark." Write the word on your journal paper.
5. Read the whole story to yourself. Write any words you cannot pronounce and I will help you with them later.
6. Do you remember the little metal boxes I gave you for storing the names of new words you have learned? If there are any words in the

story which are new to you, write them on the slips of paper and put them in your box.

The Use of Bibliotherapy

Many innovative teachers of young gifted children utilize many types of trade books to help them understand their feelings. Nancy Larrick[17] analyzed several thousand poems, letters, and short prose pieces from children and came to the conclusion that parents don't take time to listen to them. She notes that reading books aloud to children (such as *Mine for Keeps, The Summer of the Swans,* and *My Brother Steven is Retarded*) may help to build a warm personal relationship which a given child needs. Talking about the story may lead to a discussion of situations which are frustrating and perhaps downright threatening.

Gifted pupils may use the information found in the selections to help other children who have certain needs. They may wish to review the books for the benefit of the total class.

Interest Centers

One of the most fascinating learning activities for gifted primary children is the involvement and active use of interest centers which have carefully constructed by the teacher to meet the interest and grade levels of the pupils. The centers may be constructed on large tables for permanent use such as various lessons dealing with fire safety or health habits. Others may focus on various seasonal interests for a short period of time and involve holidy and weather topics. Each center should include a variety of interesting and challenging pieces of print media which will arouse the curiosity and desire of the pupil to secure the maximum amount of educational stimulation from the center.

In every case the goals of the interest center should be well planned and integrated with all of the other regular curricular activities which are ongoing in the classroom. The directions for involvement in the center should be constructed to insure a minimum of reading comprehension problems. If experiments are required in a science interest center, all materials for completing the challenges should be readily available at the center.

Many young able readers are extremely fascinated and interested in audiovisual and computer equipment. Accordingly, a well constructed social studies interest center relating to early pioneers may have films, filmstrips, film loops, and computer assisted software programs available which will serve to build the child's firm understanding of the problems encountered by the people as they traveled westward. To insure a continued, sustained level of interest, the media materials should be changed frequently. There are numerous suggestions with respect to computer software which are included in the appendices section of this volume.

Creative Desk Games

Young gifted readers find creative game activities to be interesting and stimulating if they challenge and inspire instead of seeming drill-like and repetitive. For example, in the area of word attack, the teacher may wish to structure an activity sheet with items such as the following.

1. Change the vowel and write a new word.

can't	*Mike*	*fun*	*some*	*put*
(cent)	(make)	(fan)	(same)	(pit)

2. Add another vowel to make another word that you know.

mat	*sit*	*bat*	*din*	*led*
(mate)	(site)	(bate)	(dine)	(lead)

3. Find the number of vowels in the following sentences.

   The red flag moved in the wind.   _____
   We went fishing yesterday.   _____
   Read your book before class.   _____
   Buy some paper for our school.   _____
   We will leave tomorrow.   _____

4. Read this story. Draw a circle around the words that have a long vowel sound.

   I ate a piece of cake. Mother baked the cake today. She said we could not have another bite this week.

5. Look at the underlined words in the first column. Circle a word which follows that rhymes with it.

big	mat	bit	pig	cat
turn	note	bat	folk	burn
flew	blew	went	little	send
lull	bread	mull	bend	nimble

In addition to the activities which are listed in the previous sections, the teacher may wish to employ the use of several of the periodicals and instructional materials which are noted in Appendices A and C.

EFFECTIVE PARENT-TEACHER RELATIONSHIPS

The establishment of a close working relationship between the teacher and parents of the primary gifted child is absolutely vital if significant reading growth is to take place. Though there are many actions which a teacher can undertake to promote worthwhile and wholesome relations, the following suggestions have been proven to be especially helpful and useful.

1. Compile monthly progress charts of reading skill progress and submit them to parents for their perusal and study. The data supplied should indicate (a) areas of significant growth; (b) skills which need additional practice, and (c) precise recommendations for parents to help their children improve general reading competencies.
2. Provide information papers for parents entitled "Your Child's Reading Program." Included in the narrative should be information relative to the body of skills emphasized, the names and types of materials employed, and recommendations with regard to supplementary books and other materials which may be borrowed from a library or purchased at a local bookstore.
3. Supply each parent with an informative newsletter at the beginning of the school year. Include in the publication a list of suggestions which are helpful to all children in general and gifted children in particular. The following items may be appropriate for such a newsletter.
   (a) Encourage your child to read aloud to you the parts of a book or story which are especially serious, humorous, and/or unusual.
   (b) Demonstrate that you are a good role model for your child by reading a variety of print media in his or her presence.
   (c) Read to your child aloud from five to twenty minutes a day depending upon the nature of the material read and the attention and learning level of your son or daughter.
   (d) Follow the oral reading with a non-threatening discussion of some of the main ideas, parts he or she liked best, and why the book was interesting.
   (e) Help your child pronounce any words that he or she might not know. Go over the words later and review them for reinforcement and enrichment.
4. Send a letter home with each child inviting parents to act as paraprofessionals on a regularly scheduled basis in the classroom. In this manner the parent could witness, firsthand, the degree of

ability of his or her child and gain professional techniques for challenging able learners in such important skill areas as word attack, comprehension, vocabulary, and oral reading. The school environment also provides for on-hands examination of enrichment print and electronomic media that may be purchased from a commercial business for extension skill development at home.

5. The parent-teacher conference provides a unique setting for an interchange of ideas for further enrichment and growth activities for the young gifted child. Specific recommendations should be made that are practical, reasonable, and easy to complete. The type and nature of the strategies should take into account the parent's background of experience and the amount of time available in the home environment for undertaking and completing the recommended plans.

In conclusion, while some parents may not assume enough responsibility for helping their children with reading lessons at home, a large and significant group of parents exhibit a genuine willingness to cooperate with the teacher in helping the pupil. A cooperative relationship which is built between parents and teachers is an important bridge for building positive attitudes toward reading by the child.

SUMMARY

For the young gifted child to enjoy maximum growth in reading, it is necessary to examine the learner's total competencies in the area of readiness and the factors which may be responsible for success (or lack of) in reading development. There are numerous ways for evaluating a young child's present achievement level such as competency charts, informal evaluation sheets, teacher observation, and anecdotal and cumulative records. Teachers may utilize several important strategies for enlarging the skill levels of the young child such as the language experience approach, bibliotherapy, and creative desk games. An effective relationship that is established between the parent and teacher is extremely valuable for helping to establish maximum reading growth patterns.

REFERENCES

1. Terman, Lewis M. and Maud A. Merrill. *Stanford-Binet Intelligence Scale: Manual for The Third Edition Form L-M.* Boston, Houghton Mifflin Company, 1960, p. 5.
2. Morphett, Mabel V. and Carleton Washburne, "When Should Children Begin To Read?" *Elementary School Journal,* 37 (March, 1937), pp. 498–508.

3. Swaby, Barbara E. R. *Teaching and Learning Reading, A Pragmatic Approach.* Boston, Little, Brown and Company, 1984, p. 121.

4. Harris, Larry A. and Carl B. Smith, *Reading Instruction Diagnostic Teaching In The Classroom.* New York, Macmillan Publishing Company, 1986, pp. 111–112.

5. Nila, Sister Mary, O.S.F., "Foundations of A Successful Reading Program," *Education,* 73 (May, 1953), pp. 543–555.

6. Stanovich, Keith E., Anne E. Cunningham and Dorothy J. Feeman, "Intelligence, Cognitive Skills, and Early Reading Progress," *Reading Research Quarterly* 3 (Spring, 1984), pp. 278–303.

7. Aukerman, Robert C. and Louise R. Aukerman. *How Do I Teach Reading?* New York, John Wiley and Sons, 1981, p. 53.

8. Harris, Albert J. and Edward R. Sipay. *How To Increase Reading Ability* (7th Edition). New York, Longman, 1980, p. 29.

9. Ekwall, Eldon E. *Psychological Factors In The Teaching of Reading.* Columbus, Charles E. Merrill Publishing Company, 1973, p. 62.

10. Farr, Roger and Nancy Roser. *Teaching A Child To Read.* New York, Harcourt Brace Jovanovich, Inc., 1979, p. 93.

11. Cohen, Ruth, "Remedial Training of First Grade Children with Visual Perceptual Retardation," *Educational Horizons,* 45 (1966–67), pp. 60–63.

12. Wingert, Roger C., "Evaluation of a Readiness Training Program," *The Reading Teacher,* 22 (January, 1969), pp. 325–28.

13. Harris and Smith, op. cit., p. 127.

14. Ramsey, Wallace, "Which School System Gets The Best Results in Reading?" *Journal of Reading Behavior,* Vol. I (Summer, 1969), pp. 74–80.

15. Preston, Ralph C., "Reading Achievement of German Boys and Girls Related to Sex of Teacher," *The Reading Teacher,* 32 (February, 1979), pp. 521–26.

16. Rubin, Dorothy. *Teaching Elementary Language Arts* (2nd Edition). New York, Holt, Rinehart and Winston, 1980, p. 120.

17. Larrick, Nancy. *A Parent's Guide To Children's Reading* (5th Edition). Philadelphia, The Westminster Press, 1982, p. 123.

CHAPTER IV

READING INSTRUCTION IN THE CONTENT AREAS FOR GIFTED INTERMEDIATE PUPILS

Reading is considered by educational specialists to be a process which should be promoted in all content areas. The basic skills of word attack, comprehension, and vocabulary should be taught as a regular and natural part of the social studies, science, and mathematics curriculum. All of the language arts areas (reading, writing, speaking, and listening) must be emphasized at all grade levels according to numerous surveys that have been conducted regarding the public's view of American public education.

The intermediate gifted child can be helped substantially to enlarge and enrich all of the major components of the total reading act. In order for a teacher to be of maximum service to the pupil, many principles and procedures of reading instruction must be understood and integrated into content area instruction. To supply this information, the following topics are discussed in this chapter: competencies required for reading content materials; meeting the reading needs of the gifted in the content areas; the five-step approach for reading content lessons; and extended reading activities for the gifted and talented student. A summary of the topics with a list of appropriate references conclude this important chapter.

COMPETENCIES REQUIRED FOR READING CONTENT MATERIALS

There are many pertinent competencies which are needed if the learner is to be successful in reading content materials. Accordingly, one of the first procedures to undertake in the teaching-learning process is to observe and assess the strengths of each pupil through the use of formal and informal devices. The evaluative steps will serve to supply the teacher with information such as the following: present instructional reading level; depth and nature of speaking, reading, and writing vocabularies; level of silent reading comprehension; and resource reading skill competencies. Each teacher can be of much help to the gifted learner if he or she understands the kinds of skills needed to insure that maximum advancement is realized. The competencies listed in the following sections were secured from observing hundreds of gifted pupils in classroom settings, interviews with teachers, administrators, and reading specialists.

A. *The gifted reader must learn to develop a flexible reading rate that will allow for detailed, average, skimming, and scanning speeds to be applied when details, main ideas, and brief concepts are to be remembered.* Many adults and pupils of various ages labor under the false belief that there is one best reading speed and that, regardless of purpose or objective, they can read all material in a uniform manner. In some cases they have been influenced by speed reading adherents and feel they are compelled to glance at all reading matter at a rate of hundreds of words per minute. Many reading specialists believe *that one cannot read any faster than the material can be comprehended.*

For example, if the reader wishes to read and remember, *word by word,* the preamble to the Constitution of the United States must be read and comprehended in a slow, deliberate manner. Conversely, if one needs to find if elephants are discussed in a volume about zoos, a mere scanning of the table of contents and the index at a rate exceeding 1,000 words per minute may be appropriate. There is no one best speed to use for all types of reading due to the fact that the reader must remember to maintain a two-way avenue of communication with the author.

Teachers should use direct instructional strategies to teach gifted readers that there are four rather distinct reading rates. They are as follows:

1. *Detailed reading* is the type of reading required when the learner reads at less than 125 words per minute and tries to remember a large number of facts and figures.
2. *Average* rate reading is useful for finding a few specific facts and entails reading from 125 to 400 words per minute.
3. *Skimming* at speeds from 400 to 2,000 words a minute is employed when the goal is to gain an impression of the general gist of a body of material.
4. *Scanning* is much faster than skimming since the pupil is glancing over the print in excess of 2,000 words a minute and desires to find and remember a single piece of information.

B. *The alert learner must have a practical knowledge of where to find and how to make use of various resource materials which may be needed for writing reports related to content lessons.* The gifted child should be prompted to read widely in special resource books such as the *World Almanac, Reader's Guide to Periodical Literature,* and various specialized encyclopedias. The teacher should be sure that special directions are given relative to the location of such materials. Motivational techniques and a system of awards should be established to encourage the use of resource volumes. In every case, the latest editions of each source should be available to insure that the student is studying and evaluating the best available information.

C. *One of the most significant goals of the reading program for gifted pupils is that of constructing a substantial and useful vocabulary.* Most able intermediate children are enthusiastic with regard to pronouncing and learning how to use many new words. They want to impress their friends and relatives by speaking and writing the new words. Teachers should place emphasis on helping the student enlarge skill development in all of the five general types of vocabulary: listening, speaking, reading, writing, and potential. Detailed information regarding the nature of these vocabularies along with suggested teaching strategies can be found in another volume by the author.[1]

D. *Gifted children need to develop the skill of understanding and correlate a large number of unrelated facts, principles, and concepts which may be presented in a unit or chapter of a content book.* In a social studies chapter, for example, the authors may mention as many as ten different U.S. presidents who had very different policies and experiences. The important relationships which should be developed and understood constitute a significant task for any reader. To gain facility in accomplishing these objectives requires some careful instruction and counsel on the part of the teacher. Outlines and study guides should be provided to help pupils make a distinction between facts and concepts that are important and those which are not. Helping the learner to establish definite and clear purposes for reading is vital. The questions or purposes may originate with the teacher and/or pupil or may be suggested by the author(s) of the text and resource books that are utilized.

E. *Pupils must develop the proficiency to distinguish between fact and opinion and identify numerous propaganda techniques as they appear in various print and electronic media.* The gifted learner is normally very proficient in the mastery of word attack and comprehension skills; however, in some cases, he or she displays difficulty in dealing with critical reading tasks which demand that the reader separate fact from opinion. Many young people (as well as adults) are too prone to accept everything they read as being the absolute truth. They need to gain a thorough understanding that the thoughts and statements included in editorials and many articles in newspapers and popular journals are merely the opinions of various writers and may or may not be documented truth. Specific teaching suggestions related to critical reading are described in a later section of this chapter.

F. *One of the most important skills to be developed by the gifted reader is that of summarizing and organizing a body of data which has been collected from a number of sources.* During the course of study and investigation in one or more of the content areas, a typical student frequently encounters large segments of data that require a great amount of organization for use in reports and papers. Training in the formation of appropriate outlining and study techniques is necessary if a student is to become proficient in this skill. He or she should have a clear understanding of additional resources which may be available for clarification of difficult concepts that may be encountered in regular content books.

MEETING THE READING NEEDS OF THE GIFTED IN THE CONTENT AREAS

Teachers have numerous responsibilities with regard to helping insure that each child gains maximum benefits from the reading assignments which are undertaken in the content areas. With precision instruction, each learner can increase vocabulary, enhance comprehension skills, and build a body of knowledge that encompasses many different content areas. The following are some suggestions which are pertinent for organizing and implementing a reading program in the content areas that meets the needs of the especially gifted and talented learner.

Enlarge Vocabulary in Every Lesson.

Finn[2] notes that a heavy load of new vocabulary is one of the greatest challenges in content reading. Teaching vocabulary in the content areas often means teaching the content area plus word recognition. Word recognition and structure are involved since much technical and specialized vocabulary consist of consciously invented words. The use of "mapping" may be employed which involves the placement of a word on the greenboard and then drawing lines and circles to related words which the pupils may think about.

Help students learn how to study a textbook in the proper manner. Each source which is studied has certain distinct characteristics which must be understood if complete understanding is to take place. It is the opinion of Zintz and Maggart[3] that teachers should provide guidance and help for students in locating information; organizing facts after they are found; interpreting visual information such as those found on maps, graphs, charts, and pictures; and applying the information after it has been learned. Additionally, they need to be trained to gain facility in following written directions, organize information so that it can be remembered, and take tests successfully. The gifted child will be able to secure and remember important segments of information from a textbook if the table of contents, index, chapter titles and subtopics are thoroughly explained. The purpose and nature of the preface, appendices, and reference sections should be understood. The value of giving close attention to underlined and bold-type words is vital.

Apply readability formulas to materials used by gifted children to help insure that there is a match between the instructional reading level of the pupil and the difficulty level of the print media being used in a class. Many publishers supply readability data; however, some do not. If the readability information is missing, the teacher needs to apply a reputable formula such as the *SMOG*, *Fry*, or *Dale-Chall* instruments for this purpose. At the present time one can utilize computer software programs for finding the readability level of a given material. One of the most popular programs is the READABILITY PROGRAM (Micropower and Light Company) which has the capacity for employing the use of nine separate formulas including the Dale-Chall and eight others. It is imperative to understand that any readability formula will only yield the approximate level, not the exact level, of difficulty. Indeed, using different readability formulas on the same material can produce different results.[4] The gifted intermediate pupil should be supplied with many choices of reading matter at and above his or her instructional reading level. (For the purposes of this volume, **instructional reading level** is defined as that level where a given pupil can read orally with 95 to 97 percent accuracy and demonstrate at least 75 percent proficiency in silent reading comprehension.) Able readers at the intermediate level may be able to read and comprehend books which have estimated readability levels as high as Grades 9–10.

Provide gifted readers in the content areas with a large amount of diverse and interesting reading materials. These children typically have many reading and research interests and therefore the sole use of one or two basic instructional texts will not suffice. They need easy access to the school library where they can locate and check out books, magazines, and special source books of their choice. Many of the materials noted in the appendices section of this volume may be suitable for this purpose.

Evaluate the reading skill levels of all gifted readers at frequent intervals to determine if each is achieving at his/her potential level. Evaluation consists of all types of techniques and tests which may be utilized to help the teacher understand the approximate instructional needs of the learner. Included in such a program are commercial tests, informal teacher-made tests, observation, and effective communication with each student. For example, the *Gates-MacGinitie Reading Test,* Levels D and E (Riverside) may be utilized by measuring basic vocabulary and comprehension skills. If an individual reading instrument is needed, one may choose to use the *Gates-McKillop-Horowitz Tests* (Teachers College Press). This test evaluates competencies in oral reading, word attack, visual form of words, auditory blending and discrimination, spelling, and writing.

Numerous informal measures such as the subjective reading inventory and cloze test may be appropriate. One of the major aspects to remember is to analyze *all* of the results obtained from *all* evaluation measures before making curricular plans for a given child.

Help pupils with the competencies necessary for pronouncing and understanding the hundreds of new and difficult words which are encountered. Gifted students should be challenged to read a variety of new books, magazines, and other print media. For example, in the areas of science and mathematics, pupils may encounter such difficult words as "photosynthesis," "hypotenuse," and "chemical." Unfortunately, many textbook authors assume that the reader can pronounce and understand the meanings of the words. Teachers should build the concept with pupils that the glossary, dictionary, and other resources should be used if proper understanding of such words is to be realized. Word study including the analysis of word parts and the meaning of certain Latin derivatives may be helpful.

Guide gifted students in achieving new reading competencies in order that they might meet their potential level of learning. One of the important goals of any instructor is that of helping all students reach a reading achievement which is commensurate with the number of years of school attended and their approximate intelligence quotient. Two reading authorities, Bond and Tinker,[5] constructed a reading expectancy formula in which they assume that the I.Q., is in one respect, an index of learning and therefore the reading potential of a student can be calculated by multiplying the individual's I.Q. times the number of years in school (not counting kindergarten) and adding the number 1.0. For example, if Marie has an I.Q. of 150 and is at the beginning of the fifth grade, she should be reading at the seventh grade level.

When employing a formula of this nature, one should remember that a reading expectancy score might be a useful component in the overall evaluation process; however, reading expectancy, like other indices can be in error and therefore should not be interpreted in isolation from other factors.[6] In addition to the Bond and Tinker formula, a teacher would be wise to consider other aspects such as environmental conditions, physical and mental health, and recommendations from previous teachers and other professionals.

Present purposes for reading in order that the able learner may improve overall comprehension and have goals which are related to his or her interests. One of the leading causes of ineffective comprehension is lack of purpose for reading. Gifted students need much experience in reading for information which involves critical and creative endeavors. Teachers need to pose such questions as the following:

1. From what you have read in Chapter 3, do you think the following statement is a *fact* or *opinion?*
   The leading cause of automobile accidents is excessive speed.
2. Would you have been afraid to ride in a covered wagon during the westward movement to California?

It is important to remember that there is no one definite answer which is demanded for these types of questions. Instructors need to be willing to accept any logical response which an able pupil may offer.

Provide gifted students at the intermediate grade level with special motivation to read widely in many types and kinds of print media. Lessons and activities need to be planned which encourage pupils to use a number of different sources for locating information when preparing class projects and papers. They need an opportunity to succeed and receive intrinsic awards of feeling that a substantial assignment has been completed. It would be desirable to have them empathize with literary characters, be delighted with the exposition of some historical event or scientific enterprise, chuckle or weep inwardly with a poet, and respond in other personally satisfying ways to printed material.[7] Some learners respond well to tangible awards such as noting their name on a reading honor roll or certificate which has been issued for outstanding achievement. Hopefully, the awards received by able students for reading skills improvement should be sufficient for motivating them to achieve at progressively more advanced levels of achievement.

Present lessons and activities which entail the use of several different types of learning modalities. As Lapp and Flood[8] emphasize, students learn in many ways. The instructor needs to offer a variety of learning activities that will meet the needs of all of the students enrolled. The identification of preferred modalities should be made for each learner. These data would require the teacher in each content area to possess a variety of teaching materials that would be useful for those able pupils who prefer to learn through the use of the visual, auditory, and kinesthetic methods. The many kinds of computer software mentioned in the appendices section may be viable techniques for those students who learn best through the use of visual techniques. One of the most efficient methods of determining preferred learning modality is observing the student at work and evaluating various learning traits through the use of such commercial instruments as the *Illinois Test of Psycholinguistic Abilities* (Western Psychological Services), *Bender Motor Gestalt* (Psychological Corp.), *Wepman Auditory Discrimination Test* (Western Psychological Services) and *Frostig Test of Visual Perception* (Publishers Test Service).

Relate the school experiences and assignments with the life experiences of the able learner to help insure a sustained level of interest. Reading and concomitant learning can be held at a sustained, high level when the pupil has the understanding that there is a direct relationship between his or her future goals and the current assignments. Accordingly, the activities planned for gifted pupils should be purposeful, interesting, and correspond to their needs in light of their backgrounds of experience. Extended lessons from duplicated, drill-type activities, should be avoided since they may lack proper challenge and correlation to a student's instructional reading level and general interests.

Pace reading activities for gifted readers at a rate that is related to their level of reading proficiency and attention span. Many efficient learners complete assignments at a much more rapid rate than the average to below-average reader. Some instructors have the challenge "of finding enough for them to do." Unfortunately, a few instructors have the impression that the best way to teach gifted children is to give them four pages of arithmetic problems to complete while the remainder of the class is assigned two pages. If this is standard policy, the truly gifted child finds that is is best to avoid indications of giftedness in order to escape completing an endless array of meaningless "assignments."

Pacing activities for these children involves the careful planning of individualized challenging lessons which are inspiring and helpful. The date of completion of various assignments should be realistic and based on several factors such as available working time and resource materials which may be in the classroom.

As noted in the previous section, there are several procedures and strategies which an intermediate teacher should undertake if the gifted pupil's instructional needs are to be met. Completing these plans helps to insure that each learner reaches his or her level of maximum potential and maintains a high level of motivation and enthusiasm for learning. The major emphasis in all such programs should be that of individualizing a program for the student which will help maximize reading growth; increase reading speed, vocabulary, and comprehension; and experience reading activities from a wide variety of sources. The reading program for the gifted learner must be clearly distinguished from that which is planned and executed for the average learner. Learning rates and preferred modalities must be considered to help insure the avoidance of boredom and possible anti-social behavior. School experiences for the gifted must be made satisfying and profitable for the child if the ultimate goals of success in school and life endeavors are to be fully realized.

THE FIVE-STEP APPROACH FOR
READING CONTENT LESSONS

Most content books are organized typically with a series of chapters that contain a large number of facts, figures, and concepts in a limited amount of space. All students, especially those who are able, need a well-designed and carefully formulated plan for reading and remembering the most important segments of information which are presented. The introduction and use of a reading-study plan or formula is both practical and useful for intermediate grade pupils.

The most commonly utilized formula employed by educators is the SQ3R[9] plan which calls for the pupil to survey the material to be read; devise questions or purposes for reading; read the material silently;

recite the answers to the questions; and review the information on both a short-term and long-term basis. Duffy and Roehler[10] believe that the technique is very systematic and works well and involves the readers in establishing purposes for reading, allows them to get a feel for the text through an initial survey, encourages reading to confirm or disprove the predictions embodied in the questions, and promotes the habit of checking to make sure that predictions have indeed been confirmed.

George and Evelyn Spache[11] contend that the separate steps of the SQ3R seem profitable to students because effective previewing is taught to learners, they use it, and their comprehension is definitely improved. Shepard[12] observes that teachers have found that students need not only to be instructed in the method, but also shown its value. If they read two comparable selections, one by their usual method and the other using the SQ3R approach, and are quizzed for recall, they will usually see that they have greater recall and understanding with the SQ3R.

The following is a detailed description of how Robinson's SQ3R plan might be applied in a content lesson involving the reading of a chapter of an intermediate social studies book dealing with the Westward movement which took place in the mid-1840's.

I. *Readiness or Survey Stage*

At the beginning of the lesson, the teacher asks the pupils to survey or scan the chapter title, sub-topics, and italicized words to gain an overall impression regarding the nature and kind of subjects to be studied. Students may be asked if they have ever read books or viewed movies related to pioneer life. The teacher's discussion should have the major goal of "selling" the importance of the topics to the learners.

New vocabulary words can be introduced *in context* to enhance meaning and understanding. The following words may be presented.

> Some travelers wanted newer, more *fertile* land. *Settlements* grew up at railroad and ranching villages. By 1870, many *deposits* of gold and other precious metals had been found in California, Idaho, Colorado, and Nevada.

II. *Question or Purpose Stage*

Since one of the major reasons for a low level of comprehension ability is lack of purpose for reading, it is vital for the teacher to construct questions or purposes for a pending reading assignment. The number of questions utilized and formed should depend on the age and learning level of the pupil. For intermediate pupils who are expected to read five pages from a social studies text, the teacher may wish to pose three or four questions. The questions assigned should be constructed from all four of the comprehension levels. During the study of the *Westward Movement* the teacher may wish to use questions such as the following for the reading assignment:

Literal: In what state was gold discovered?
Interpretive: Give one reason why many people decided to join the caravan of wagons headed west.
Critical: Read the following statements. If they are *facts,* write "yes." If they are merely *ideas* or *opinions,* write "no."

_____ 1. The Indians did not like the pioneers who came near them.
_____ 2. Many of the people who went to California were in search of gold.
_____ 3. Most pioneers were not brave.

Creative: If you had been living in Pennsylvania or New York in 1849, would you have joined the hundreds of people who went west? Why or why not?

The previous questions should be duplicated and handed to the pupils to answer immediately after they have had a chance to complete the silent reading. A classwide oral discussion relating to the possible responses to the questions may be held. The answers to the literal and interpretive questions should be somewhat similar; however, the responses from gifted intermediate readers will be quite varied for the critical and creative questions. Any reasonable or logical answer should be accepted in order to motivate the pupil to extend his or her creative reading endeavors or goals.

III. *Silent Reading Stage*

After carefully studying and evaluating the various questions and purposes, the pupils should read silently print media materials which are likely to contain the answers to the questions. For most students these items would consist primarily of the adopted text while gifted readers should be encouraged not only to read the text but to utilize selected resource books found in the classroom and school libraries. Encyclopedias as well as historical fiction and non-fictional volumes at upper grade and secondary reading levels may prove to be challenging and provocative for able intermediate readers.

The readers may like to participate in book conferences with the teacher and share resource reading materials through the use of oral reviews before the entire class. The use of personal illustrations may accompany the reports. The concepts obtained from the material read during the silent reading stage may serve as a basis for the construction of a bulletin board display, learning center, or a diorama.

By observing the pupils while reading silently, impressions may be gained relative to attention span, time on task, reading rate, and interest in the reading act. Individual conversations with various gifted learners may provide opportunities for the teacher to recommend techniques relating to such aspects as reading rate improvement, comprehension skills, and time management skills.

IV. *Discussion Stage*

An oral discussion should take place following the silent reading activity to react to the answers or responses regarding the questions which were formulated in Stage II. The responses offered by the students should provide a clue concerning each learner's level of competency for all of the stages of comprehension. Particular attention should be given to gifted readers to assess the degree of proficiency obtained in both critical and creative comprehension skills. If the pupils encounter difficulty with these kinds of questions, additional help and instruction may be needed. Able learners need to be motivated to achieve at maximum levels in the more advanced levels of comprehension and thinking skills.

V. *Culminating Activity Stage*

In the content areas, the instructor needs to make a planned, conscious effort to correlate all of the segments and concepts introduced which will result in an integrated body of data and knowledge that is easy to understand and remember. Relating the events of one historical age to another helps able learners to realize that the present condition of the human race is naturally dependent on what has happened in previous decades and centuries.

In social studies various teaching strategies such as bulletin boards, time-lines, charts, and graphs can be utilized to help pupils draw appropriate relationships between and among various events which affect current events. Students who have special artistic talents may wish to create murals, posters, and hallway displays to demonstrate their overall understanding of a given unit which has been studied. They may also wish to write a script of a play or a drama for use by a selected group of pupils in making a special presentation for parents when a unit of study in science or social studies has been completed.

EXTENDED READING ACTIVITIES FOR THE GIFTED AND TALENTED STUDENT

In addition to the five-step approach described in the previous section for principal use in traditional content subjects, there are numerous other meaningful reading activities in the areas of creative writing, vocabulary, and comprehension which can be utilized in a number of situations during the school day. The activities described in this segment of the chapter are especially designed to challenge and motivate gifted and talented children to maximize their growth of reading skill components and reach their ultimate potential. The use of a given procedure should be undertaken with one or more pupils after the following aspects are considered: (a) age of the learner; (b) background of experience; (c) preferred learning modality; (d) level of motivation; and (e) instructional needs. A variety of activities should be selected to help insure a high level of interest and a healthy competitive atmosphere among the total class membership.

Creative Writing Activities

1. Smith[12] suggests that social studies teachers can utilize the study of the Declaration of Independence to encourage students to engage in an activity such as the following:

> You have read that Adams and Franklin made some changes in Jefferson's draft of the Declaration. Pretend that the three of them have met to discuss those changes. Who would begin the conversation? How might the history of this nation have been changed by the meeting? Write three or four paragraphs explaining your responses to these questions.

2. A very interesting creative writing activity is to provide pupils with the *last* sentence of an essay. Ask them to create a possible story or

selection which may logically precede the final sentence. The following are possible sentences which may be utilized for this purpose.

  a. And that is why my bathtub was filled with iced tea.
  b. That monkey must be the funniest animal in the world.
  c. Don't ever offer a crocodile a treat unless you mean it.
  d. My dad says he will never paint our house again.
  e. I will sit on the top row of seats the next time I go to a football game.
  f. If you want good luck, be sure to carry a rabbit's foot in your pocket.

3. The use of bulletin boards and pictures may stimulate students to want to compose creative stories about the items they have viewed. For example, a teacher may display a series of three or four pictures that illustrate a short sequence of events which took place in an imaginary story. Ask pupils to complete the story in essay form in any manner which they deem to be logical and interesting. As a matter of interest, invite students to volunteer to read their selections aloud.

4. Instructors may wish to play a tape-recording of an instrumental music selection such as "New York, New York" or "Home On The Range." Pupils should be invited to listen to the selection and describe how the music makes them feel. Mr. Smithson, a sixth grade teacher, played a recording of "Pomp and Circumstance" by Elgar. Hershal, a talented pupil, wrote the following essay.

> There is a large, enthusiastic audience of parents and friends of the graduating class. Dozens of people are marching to the front of the huge auditorium to receive their diplomas. There are several distinguished people sitting on the stage—one is Dr. Maynard, our superintendent. In a few years I hope to march to the front of the auditorium for my diploma. That seems like a long time from now.

5. Predicting outcomes provides a unique opportunity for gifted pupils to engage in creative writing endeavors. A teacher may choose to compose the following partial selection and duplicate it for distribution to the group of pupils.

Surprise at the Circus

> It was one o'clock in the afternoon and Bill, Mark, and Jerry were walking to the Civic Auditorium to see a performance by the Ringling Brothers, Barnum and Bailey Circus. As they reached the front door they were greeted by a clown who escorted them to their seats in the first row of the building. After a drum roll by the old drummer, the monkeys started racing around the room and jumping through the large plastic hoops. One of them missed the hoop

and flew through the air toward me. I turned to one side and _____

_____

_____

_____

6. Meaningful exercises which emphasize cause and effect relationships provide meaningful situations for reinforcing creative writing skills. Burns and Roe[13] recommend that a teacher should select a book or story which contains an obvious cause-and-effect situation. The selection can be read in its entirety or a certain portion can be utilized. The pupils can also read the designated selection for themselves. At the conclusion of the reading, they can be asked what would be the effect on the rest of the story if a certain event had not taken place. One may ask what would have happened in the selection *Heidi* if Peter had not pushed Klara's wheelchair down the side of the mountain.

Particular emphasis should be made to impress gifted readers that their responses will no doubt be varied and thus, no one definitive, precise statement is expected or demanded. Any logical and reasonable explanation will be accepted as long as the effect is a plausible product of the cause which has been described.

7. Perceiving correct relationships among a group of words lends practice in building both vocabulary and creative writing skill components. As Selma Herr[14] suggests, a teacher may prepare groups of words which have a relationship. The students are to write another word that is related to the other four words.

EXAMPLES:
a. red blue yellow white   _____
b. football basketball hockey soccer   _____
c. pears peaches apples grapes   _____
d. Chevrolet Oldsmobile Ford Dodge   _____
e. Kansas Iowa Illinois Delaware   _____
f. fast quick rapid swift   _____
g. said answered spoke replied   _____
h. car airplane train bicycle   _____
i. meat potatoes pudding salad   _____
j. pencil paper eraser ink   _____

8. One of the most productive avenues for the promotion of creative writing endeavors for gifted and able children is the planning, writing, and production of a school newspaper. Some of the responsibilities which may be appropriate include the following:

A. SELECTING the articles for each edition along with an estimate of the amount of space which may be needed for the article.
B. WRITING the articles with particular attention given to precise details, descriptive language which is interesting and stimulating, and vocabulary which is at the correct level of difficulty for the reading audience.
C. EDITING the selections with the view of trying to eliminate duplication, difficult language, and uneven sentences. The child chosen as editor will have the overall responsibility for insuring that the final copy is in good order and is ready for publication by an agreed upon deadline.
D. PROOFREADING the final copy to help insure that misspelled words have been eliminated and all sentences are complete and easily read.
E. COMPILING appropriate headlines and subtitles should be carefully undertaken to assure that the relationship between headlines and copy is clear and positive. The headlines should attract the reader's interest but not reveal the complete story. A headline should not mislead, and it must conform to the allowable space.

Further information about how to create your own classroom newspaper can be usually obtained from the educational coordinator of any large city daily paper.

Vocabulary Activities

If the gifted intermediate reader is to progress at a maximum level with regard to the total act of reading, it is vital for him or her to experience steady, daily growth in all of the five general types of vocabulary . . . listening, speaking, reading, writing, and potential. There are vocabulary terms which are unique to the various content areas. For example, in the area of science, the learner may encounter such words as "lanthanum," "ornithologist," and "rotifer." As noted earlier, these words must be introduced and taught during the readiness stage of the five-step approach to teaching reading in the content areas. In addition to the regular lesson opportunities for vocabulary development, there are numerous classroom activities which may be correlated with the total curricular offerings during the school day. Descriptions of several of these lessons are given below.

1. One of the major complexities of the English language is the fact that various words may have the same word element but have widely

varying meanings. Students can gain practice in this skill by completing an exercise similar to the following.

Directions. The first column contains words with the same word element, "love." In the second column is a list of scrambled definitions which fit the words. Write the number of the definition to the left of the word which matches the definition of that word.

_____ a. lovebird	1. not loving
_____ b. lovefeast	2. very pleasing and delightful
_____ c. loveless	3. beauty
_____ d. loveliness	4. a person who loves
_____ e. lovelorn	5. parakeet
_____ f. lovely	6. suffering as a result of love
_____ g. lover	7. banquet for promoting good feeling

2. An analogy shows or reveals the relationship of one word to another. A broad understanding of analogies helps to increase reading and speaking vocabularies of all pupils (especially gifted and able). The exercise which follows may be utilized as either an exercise or a diagnostic instrument.

Directions: Study the following analogies. Circle the word among the choices which correctly completes the analogy.

a. over: under/up	above down stop
b. sad: happy/cry	frown weep laugh
c. black: white/day	morning noon night
d. winter: summer/cold	hot cloth cool
e. mice: mouse/cow	cattle animals milk
f. sour: sweet/salt	bread table sugar
g. feet: head/roof	ceiling floor wall
h. peach: pear/Chevrolet	Ford train plane

3. *The Cloze procedure* is an excellent technique for evaluating and promoting vocabulary skills. Duplicate a passage and leave out every fifth word. Place the names of the omitted words in a scrambled list and ask the pupils to select those words which should be utilized for each of the blanks. One of the variations which may be used is to allow each pupil to write a word of their *own* choice on each of the blanks. Encourage students to read aloud their selections to demonstrate the various semantic approaches which were taken.

4. Synonym and antonym exercises challenge gifted and talented pupils to practice their abilities to define various words. A synonym exercise similar to the following may be useful.

Directions: In each of the following lines is a capitalized key word which is followed by four other words. One of the words means the same or nearly the same as the capitalized word. Circle the word which matches the meaning of the key word.

a. SPITE	heavy	grudge	nice	envy
b. RENEGADE	deserter	promise	repine	crank
c. MIRAGE	wall	river	hill	appearance
d. LIAISON	triple	connection	libel	calculate
e. HEAP	hazy	pile	infamous	triple
f. EXEMPT	promote	huge	magnify	release
g. BREACH	brace	opening	counter	ceiling
h. POSSESS	own	hearsay	mystery	wall

The study and practice of Latin prefixes and suffixes is both interesting and fascinating for able learners. An exercise similar to the following may be used for this purpose.

Directions: There are ten sentences in this lesson. Each sentence contains a blank. Under the blank is the name of a root word. Combine the root word with a prefix to form a new word which would be suitable for the blank. Use the following prefixes for this lesson: *im, mis, ex, sub, trans, con, super, tri, anti,* and *inter.*

I will try to _____ to your wishes.
  form

Every winter I put _____ in my car.
  freeze

I think I _____ my coat at school.
  placed

It is _____ for me to go at this time.
  possible

The farmers will _____ their grain.
  port

Draw a _____ at the bottom of the page.
  angle

Mike plays on an _____ football team.
  varsity

The roots had grown to the _____ of the field.
  soil

My neighbor _____ his rose bushes.
  planted

The carpenter _____ the plastic on top of the kitchen counter.
  imposed

Comprehension Activities

A major objective of any reading teacher should be that of helping pupils to gain further skills at each of the four levels of comprehension. Special emphasis should be placed on strengthening critical and creative competencies for gifted readers at the intermediate level. The following are some brief examples of exercises which may be employed with able learners for evaluating ability to remember details.

1. Supply a copy of a short story of three or four pages to each child. Use sentences taken from the selection and list three or four choices for completing the sentence properly.

Examples:

a. The reason Mary took the chocolate cake to her grandmother was to

_____

receive exercise
please her grandmother
have something to do

b. f you cross the street with a red light you _____

might get hurt
can save time
will deliver more goods

2. To test the critical reading skill levels of intermediate pupils, ask them to read a selection and then make a determination if a selected series of statements are *opinions* or *facts.*

Examples:

_____ a. People become taller as they grow older.
_____ b. Exercise and proper diet are essential for good health.

3. Drawing appropriate conclusions is a skill which should be developed with all readers. Able readers should find exercises in this component to be especially challenging and stimulating.

a. Select sentences from a reading or content area textbook and ask pupils to supply an appropriate response.

Example:

Bill was sad as he talked to Mark about the circus coming to town.
Bill was unhappy because _____

_____

b. Short examples of paragraphs taken from a social studies or science book may be copied. A multiple-choice question may be utilized to test skills in drawing conclusions.

Example:

The rich, loam soil of western Iowa provides a perfect setting for the growing of huge fields of corn. However, occasional droughts spell disaster for the unwary farmer. When farmers cannot harvest grain they _____ lose money _____ must loan money _____ buy a larger farm.

c. Select sentences from a content book and prepare questions similar to the following which will cause the able reader to think about the skills of forming appropriate conclusions.

Examples:

Could this incident have taken place near our school?
What do you think was the *real* reason why Sam and Mike did not go to the picnic?
Why was the cotton gin such an important invention?

It is important to remember several important principles when preparing reading exercises for gifted intermediate readers.

1. All exercises and activities should be based on each pupil's interest and instructional reading levels.
2. Educational strategies should always be undertaken with the view of enriching the learner's body of current knowledge as opposed to drill activities which may be utilized "to keep them busy."
3. All lessons should be designed to provide a "springboard" for encouraging the learners to expand their reading interest and competencies.

SUMMARY

If an able reader is to make satisfactory progress in reading content materials, he or she must develop certain identifiable characteristics which are described in this chapter. Instructors can meet the needs of these pupils through the use of various strategies. The enlargement of vocabulary and comprehension skill levels can be realized through the use of the five-step approach to teaching reading in the content areas. Enrichment activities such as those enumerated at the close of the chapter are very helpful for insuring maximum reading growth of pupils.

REFERENCES

1. Cushenbery, Donald C. *Improving Reading Skills in The Content Area.* Springfield, Charles C Thomas, Publisher, 1985, Chapter 4.
2. Finn, Patrick J. *Helping Children Learn to Read.* New York, Random House, 1985, pp. 218–219.

3. Zintz, Miles V. and Zelda R. Maggart. *Corrective Reading* (Fifth Edition). Dubuque, Wm. C. Brown Publishers, 1986, p. 297.

4. Heilman, Arthur W., Timothy R. Blair, and William H. Rupley. *Principles and Practices of Teaching Reading* (Sixth Edition). Columbus, Charles E. Merrill Publishing Company, 1986, p. 230.

5. Bond, Guy L., Miles A. Tinker, and Barbara B. Wasson. *Reading Difficulties, Their Diagnosis and Correction* (Fourth Edition). Englewood Cliffs, Prentice-Hall, Inc., 1979, p. 62.

6. Burns, E. "Linear Regression and Simplified Reading Expectancy Formulas," *Reading Research Quarterly,* 17, 3 (1982), p. 453.

7. Smith, Richard J. and Dale D. Johnson. *Teaching Children To Read.* Reading, Addison-Wesley Publishing Company, 1976, p. 23.

8. Lapp, Diane and James Flood. *Teaching Students To Read.* New York, Macmillan Publishing Company, 1986, p. 199.

9. Robinson, Francis P. *Effective Study* (Revised Edition). New York, Harper and Row, Inc., 1961, pp. 13–48.

10. Duffy, Gerald G. and Roehler, Laura R. *Improving Classroom Reading Instruction.* New York, Random House, 1986, p. 333.

11. Spache, George D. and Evelyn B. Spache. *Reading In The Elementary School* (Fifth Edition). Boston, Allyn and Bacon, Inc., 1986, p. 376.

12. Smith, Richard J. "Using Reading To Stimulate Creative Thinking In The Intermediate Grades," *Creative Reading For Gifted Learners* (Michael Labuda, Editor). Newark, International Reading Association, 1974, p. 57.

13. Burns, Paul C. and Betty D. Roe. *Reading Activities for Today's Elementary Schools.* Chicago, Rand McNally College Publishing Company, 1979, p. 102.

14. Selma E. Herr, *Learning Activities for Reading* (Fourth Edition). Dubuque, Wm. C. Brown Company, Publishers, 1982, p. 64.

CHAPTER V

UNDERTAKING READING STRATEGIES FOR GIFTED SECONDARY STUDENTS

U ntil recent years, identifiable reading programs for gifted students have been mostly lacking in many secondary schools. In more traditional systems, these learners were probably taught in the same manner as average pupils with some provisions for longer and more difficult assignments. The older reader must be challenged and inspired to read and learn at a maximum level in order to avoid boredom and disinterest. To establish a viable program of studies for these students, educators must be knowledgeable with regard to a number of important aspects that are discussed in this chapter.

The following topics are included in this section: reading attitudes of the gifted secondary student; principles of an effective reading curriculum for gifted secondary students; types of reading programs for gifted adolescent learners; and evaluation of secondary reading programs for able readers. A summary and a body of references conclude the chapter.

READING ATTITUDES OF THE GIFTED SECONDARY STUDENT

There are numerous and varied observed attitudes with respect to able readers at the secondary level. A thorough description of the characteristics of gifted students in general is included in Chapter I. In addition to the aspects noted in this segment, there are additional traits which are unique to secondary readers.

A recent study[1] conducted by Anderson, Tollefson, and Gilbert surveyed the attitudes toward reading and reading behaviors of gifted students in Grades 1 through 12. The Likert-type questionnaire involved 11 items which surveyed pupils' attitudes with regard to such items as reading assignments, importance of reading as an everyday activity, and reading workload. The students selected for the study had been identified as gifted students according to ability tests and had obtained composite reading achievement scores which placed them in the top 5 percent of the national norm group. The data analyzed from the investigation revealed that secondary gifted readers hold the following attitudes:

1. **Reading activity in high school is much less than at the elementary level and there is a lower level of interest in reading as a favorite leisure activity than is true with younger readers.**
2. **Assignments are easy and many are tediously long.**
3. **Reading as a hobby has a much lower value at the secondary level than is true for elementary learners. For example, only 38 percent of gifted secondary boys chose reading as a hobby.**

Another careful investigation[2] was undertaken to establish the relationship between written expression and reading in gifted adolescent readers. The research study involved 107 subjects who were enrolled in a special public school for gifted adolescents in a large northeastern city. The investigators made a statistical study of the relationship between scores obtained on the *California Achievement Test* (C.T.B.) and the *Test of Written Language* (TOWL). After analyzing the data from both instruments, the following conclusions were reached:

1. **The subjects performed well on most of the written language tasks evaluated. They scored especially well on the mechanical aspects such as handwriting and punctuation; however, they were merely adequate with regard to conveying ideas through creative writing since they had experienced little direct instruction in this skill.**
2. **For the most part, there appears to be little relationship between written language ability and reading skills.**

Instructional Challenges and Reading Attitudes

The recognition of the typical attitudes of older gifted readers requires teachers to make instructional alterations to allow learners to make maximum educational growth. The following statements serve to summarize the challenges which should be considered when teaching reading skills to the gifted learner at the junior and senior high levels.

1. Many able readers gain the impression that the reading materials provided by the teacher are too simple and thus are not challenging in terms of their ability level and current interests. A variety of materials must be offered to meet individual needs.
2. Because many able readers are seriously interested in critical and creative levels of comprehension, instructors must present reading purposes that are much broader than mere production of literal

details. These aspects might include forming significant interrelationships, tracing themes and overall topics, and analyzing the importance of the selection as a whole.

3. These students normally desire a flexible schedule with regard to reading activities and have a disdain for rigid schedules, authoritative teaching, and simplistic grading procedures which may be employed with traditional students.

4. Reading assignments provided for these students must be based from a problem-centered approach rather than a uniform, capricious exercise intended for average and/or below average readers. These students tend to learn through association rather than the simple rote memory of isolated facts and principles.

5. The reward system that works best with the able secondary reader is that which is based around intrinsic rather than extrinsic foundations. For many of these learners the knowledge that they have learned new and different information will cause them to be more creative and imaginative.

6. The able reader displays typical attitudes which exhibits feelings of imagination, creativity, and curiosity. Assignments made for these students should be structured to require abstraction and a high degree of maturity. Many of them have the impression that thin books with large pictures are "babyish." Accordingly, the secondary teacher needs to have a sizable number of reading materials available which have readability levels at the upper secondary and university levels.

7. Gifted secondary readers often prefer to present information they have found by means of oral presentations, panel discussions, and artistic projects rather than being required to submit long, detailed written reports which tend to be stifling, time-consuming, and dull.

8. It is important for secondary teachers to remember that some gifted students, particularly those with physical abilities or whose first language is not standard English, may require remedial instruction in basic skills; therefore instruction should be aimed at the completion of a skill sequence to permit learners to progress at their own rate to more advanced skills.[3]

9. Although most gifted adolescents can comprehend the vast majority of their class reading assignments, they often read at an average rate of about 250–300 words a minute. Obviously, if they are to read and assimilate the large number of pages of required reading at the forthcoming university level, they must be instructed with regard to the use of skimming and scanning techniques as described by Cushenbery in Chapter 7, *Improving Reading Skills in The Content Areas* (Charles C Thomas, 1985).

10. Able readers develop higher levels of comprehension when they

are given well defined purposes before they engage in reading large amounts of material. They must understand that gaining meaning and communicating with the author constitutes the end product of the act of reading. "Covering" material at a fast rate is not a practical objective unless it is accompanied by complete understanding of details and main ideas.

PRINCIPLES OF AN EFFECTIVE READING CURRICULUM FOR GIFTED SECONDARY STUDENTS

Instructors must remember that *reading is not a subject but a body of skills which should be introduced, taught, and reinforced at all grade levels.* This basic principle is true for all readers, especially those who are gifted and talented. To insure that all of the basic competencies are taught, students must be instructed through the use of their preferred learning modality after appropriate evaluation procedures have been utilized. The following principles should be carefully inculcated in all reading lessons and assignments.

In order to meet the exact instructional requirements of pupils on an individual basis, a careful analysis must be made of each learner's present level of reading skill development. Reading programs for all students must be individualized in order to help insure that the instructional offerings will have maximum benefit for each learner. After a person has been identified as a gifted student, an appropriate series of evaluative measures should be employed to identify his or her basic reading strengths and limitations. These strategies may include such nationally known commercial tests as *The California Reading Tests* (CTB); *Gates-MacGinitie Reading Tests* (Riverside); *Iowa Tests of Educational Development* (SRA); and *Nelson-Denny Reading Test* (Riverside). Measures such as informal reading, teacher constructed inventories, cloze tests, and structured observation procedures may be utilized. (The next chapter contains detailed information regarding the total structure of a program of reading evaluation.) An analysis sheet for each learner should be constructed to provide valuable information regarding such data as each learner's independent, instructional, and frustration reading levels; comprehension development; reading interests; preferred learning modality; and rate of reading. Studying these data will aid the teacher in selecting the most productive methods and strategies for use with each individual student.

Teachers should plan and undertake lessons which will challenge the gifted and talented reader to work at his or her maximum level when the potential or capacity reading capabilities of the student are considered. To help insure that this goal is achieved, each instructor needs to secure many different types of reading and learning materials which are representative of various subject and interest levels and designed to have high interest and informative value. (Information concerning many of these teaching tools can be found in Appendix C of this volume.) For secondary students, this practice would entail the placement of university and college level subject and resource books in the classroom and school library. Information concerning these volumes and their location should be provided for all learners, especially those who are gifted and talented.

The lessons undertaken with secondary gifted readers should be varied and provide avenues of learning that will make use of the preferred learning modalities of the learners. Each individual has a special and unique method of learning new knowledge. These modalities may include aural, visual, and kinesthetic procedures. The able visual learner may need to be exposed to a large number of books, magazines, and other print material while the use of the classroom computer may be more suitable for those students who prefer the visual modes of learning. Discovering which modality is preferred by a given student can be ascertained through informal observational techniques, certain commercial instruments, and interviews with the students.

Since most able readers are goal oriented, they need to be apprised relative to their special strengths and limitations with regard to their total body of reading skill competencies. These data can be presented through the use of organized tables and charts and oral discussion by the teacher during an individual interview. Every reader should have goals for further improvement. For the gifted secondary reader, they may consist of reading at a faster rate, improving oral and written vocabulary skills and enlargement of comprehension skills at all four levels (literal, interpretive, critical, creative).

Provisions should be made to allow each gifted reader to share and demonstrate new facts and concepts which have been gained from his or her reading activities. Some high school students may wish to participate in such activities as the debate club, student government programs, and special class demonstrations to present new information and concepts that have been recently acquired. Many gifted secondary students have an aversion to undertaking standard, non-creative writing assignments (such as book reports) since they have little opportunity to express their critical and creative ideas within the confines of such an assignment.

Opportunities should be provided for gifted secondary students to evaluate the reading instructional program which is currently being employed. Given the proper rapport between students and teachers, each learner may be asked to complete a Likert-type instrument such as the following.

	Strongly Agree			Strongly Disagree	
	1	2	3	4	5

1. I have an opportunity to read books in this class which are interesting and useful to me.
2. The textbook in this class is too "babyish."
3. Most of the assignments are too detailed.
4. The library in this school contains the kinds of books which are of much value to me in completing assignments.
5. If you read well in this class, you are awarded by the teacher with better grades.
6. The teacher spends too much time on how to pronounce and comprehend words.
7. If you are a good reader, the teacher gives you more attention than if you are a poor reader.
8. Good readers have to do more work in this class than do poor readers.

When possible, able readers may realize a higher level of success if they are involved with small group instruction activities. Burmeister[4] contends, for example, that when students have common reading achievement levels, common skill needs, or common interests, they can be grouped together. The authority believes that students in such groups can function together for a short period of time and when their goal is reached they can be disbanded. In achievement grouping, students may be scheduled together to read materials they are capable of reading while on other occasions they may be joined on the basis of interests.

TYPES OF READING PROGRAMS FOR
GIFTED ADOLESCENT LEARNERS

Construction of special reading programs for gifted secondary students is a fairly recent phenomenon. For example, Greenlaw and Moore[5] conducted a study of 251 randomly selected junior and senior high schools in 1982 and found that the percentage of schools offering accelerated reading courses was 16 percent in Grade 7; 16 percent in Grade 8; 7 percent in Grade 9; 12 percent in Grade 10; 16 percent in Grade 11; and 20 percent in Grade 12.

At the present time there are various methods and strategies being employed by educators for helping older readers reach their maximum level of success. In Chapter 2 a number of model programs for elementary pupils were described. Several of these could be altered to a degree to accommodate secondary students. In the section which follows, several kinds of curricular programs or strategies are described which may be adapted or adopted for use in given secondary schools. The program utilized will obviously depend on several factors including class size, materials available, amount of funds for new purchases, and faculty available for designing and implementing the new plans. Proper evaluation of students for purposes of initial placement and identification for enrollment in special curricular segments is vital and extremely important.

Chapter 6 of this volume is devoted to a discussion of several valuable aspects of the evaluation process including the purposes of evaluation, principles of an effective program of evaluation, standardized and informal reading tests, and methods for utilizing the results obtained from various reading evaluation instruments. Many of the volumes noted in Appendix B contain valuable suggestions for implementing secondary reading programs for gifted students. Additional suggestions for forming successful strategies for able readers can usually be obtained by consulting with the directors of local and area university reading clinics and graduate gifted programs.

General Reading Programs for Gifted Secondary Students

A. *Acceleration.* In a given secondary school which may have several language arts offerings in sequence, an able reader may be allowed to move ahead to an advanced course if he or she can demonstrate mastery of competencies required in the basic classes. Evaluation procedures for rendering these decisions may include the use of commercial and/or informal tests, recommendations of teachers, and conversations with the affected student. The accelerated class allows the learner to work with other students of similar abilities and thus provides sufficient challenge to the student to help insure motivation and interest.

B. *Classroom Enrichment.* Each teacher in the secondary content areas makes provision in his or her instructional procedures to allow gifted readers to pursue creative projects such as reporting on advanced text materials which have been read recently. The learners may also be encouraged to complete research and/or study projects which require supplementary reading from challenging resource books located in the school, city, or university libraries. Students with these abilities may also find it interesting to write human interest stories for the school or city newspaper.

C. *Special Reading and Language Arts Credit and Non-Credit Courses.* Many school administrators have found the offering of special courses for accelerated readers to be useful for those students who may have vocational goals for future academic training at a college or university. The skills learned in these courses may provide an excellent background of experience and training when undertaking the challenge of scoring at a high level on the S.A.T. test. The advanced score may allow the young person to be awarded a valuable scholarship.

The titles of courses offered should be varied and tailored to meet the needs of the students. One secondary school offered the following short courses for their able readers: "Speed Reading," "Reading for Fun and Relaxation," and "Preparing Term Papers and Special Reports." Regulations accompanying these courses required a minimum enrollment of 12 in each class and the participating student was required to have at least a 3.3 grade point average on a 4.0 scale.

D. *Pre-College Course Enrollment.* Many high school administrators have recently established programs with local universities and colleges to permit highly talented and gifted adolescents to enroll for higher education credits before receiving a high school diploma. For example, in 1980, California State University at Los Angeles first admitted very young adolescents for part-time study based on scores from the *Washington Pre-College Test.* Percentile scores assigned by comparison to the performance of high school juniors and seniors who planned to attend college were considered. These Early Entrance Program students were required to attend counseling sessions and group meetings. In 1985, eight adolescents ranging in ages from 11 to 16 attended the program.[6] Since the University of Washington and the Johns Hopkins University had already developed such programs, CSULA used their programs and models for their own endeavor. Another innovative program for gifted junior high school students was offered by Iowa State University during the summer of 1987 for 55 students, ages 13 and 14, who scored exceptionally high on the Scholastic Aptitude Test. The CYTAG program, which was modeled after one established at Duke University in 1980, allows students to enroll in concentrated, individualized courses in mathematics, biotechnology, and English. The curriculum permits the learners to advance at a rapid rate through high school levels, and in some instances, into college level work. Students were taught by members of the university faculty and teams of teaching assistants, and lived in university dormitories during the instruction. Further information concerning the CYTAG program may be obtained by writing to: Dr. Elizabeth Beck, Coordinator of Special Programs, Osborne Cottage, Iowa State University, Ames, Iowa 50011.

E. *Community Programs for Able Readers.* An innovative science program for gifted students was conducted during the summer of 1984 at Argonne National Laboratory near Chicago. The learners had a chance to read about many subjects and listen to scientists and high quality teachers. The programs lasted three weeks and involved 125 gifted students. A statistical evaluation study of the worth of the program showed that there was a substantial increase in the students' knowledge level at the close of the program.[7]

F. *Small Group Instruction.* Barbara Moller[8] is of the belief that most advanced readers need both a broad exposure to challenging works and instruction to understand a complexity of reading matter such as professional journals, research reports, and abstracts. Specially designated older students whose reading level is much above average might be grouped with a well trained teacher who can introduce the learners to new subject areas with greater proficiency through the development, application, and extension of materials. She is of the belief that this cycle of three types of assignments gives students opportunity to develop specific skills and extend their reading interests.

Small group instruction may also provide for a higher level of motivation and general interest since the instruction is fast-paced and each learner can progress at a rate which helps insure a high level of interest.

The use of learning contracts may be especially appropriate in these situations to help insure learning at a maximum rate.

G. *Peer Tutoring Programs.* The gifted and talented adolescent reader may be stimulated to increase his or her level of reading interest through a program of peer tutoring during which time the able learner is afforded the opportunity and responsibility for helping to instruct a fellow student who needs additional skill practice. As Brazell[9] notes, however, there are certain admonitions which must be remembered by educators when they establish the programs. She notes that the following selected principles may serve as appropriate criteria for constructing such programs:

1. The activity should be under the guidance of a teacher, must be structured, and constantly recognized and evaluated.
2. The tutor should participate in structured workshops for the purpose of learning what should be expected of the tutee, understanding when instructional objectives have been met, and knowing how to evaluate the degree of change of behavior in the pupil being instructed.
3. If the experience is satisfying and rewarding, one can develop very critical clients for the future teaching profession.

H. *Dramatic and Artistic Enrichment Activities Curriculum.* The superior reader who is generally thought to be gifted and talented may enjoy undertaking specific classroom activities which involve dramatizing stories, making graphic representations of a story, and constructing oral and written presentations of stories[10]. Shepherd notes that such activities may consist of aspects such as rewriting a story as a play, showing a selection in serial form, making illustrations, relating a story to the most exciting part, and rewriting an ending to a selection. Additional creative endeavors may include the construction of motivational bulletin boards for advertising new books in the library and promotion of extension reading through the advertisement of a "Read A Good Book This Week" theme through stories in the school newspaper and/or announcements over the school intercom system.

I. *Challenge Vocabulary Study Clubs.* One of the most valuable areas of study contributing to reading growth is that of vocabulary enlargement. Most secondary gifted readers are very fascinated and interested in learning the meaning and use of new and unusual words which may be a part of their regular content subject reading assignments. Some instructors invite able, interested readers to participate in a structured vocabulary study program during which time the student may wish to maintain a vocabulary notebook that contains one or more of the following aspects with regard to new words encountered: the correct pronunciation of the word, general and specialized meanings of the word, use of the word in sentences, and the origin of the word. Some students may desire to "pool" their information and compile a useful handbook of new words and meanings which may be unique to a given content area.

J. *Interest Centers for Gifted Readers.* The use of interest centers may serve as a source of motivation for able learners. Cagney and Sakiey[11] suggest, for example, that a center on history may include data relating to the work of historians and the contributions they have made. Local or state history books, old maps, newspapers, advertisements, and other kinds of historical documents· may be used for building the center. Students may wish to pursue an investigative paper and/or report and could utilize these data for documentation of various aspects of the topic.

K. *Tape-Recording and Writing Activities.* Because gifted adolescents typically have many interests, they tend to be better able to verbalize their impressions than they are to compose their thoughts by writing. One authority[12] suggests the use of the tape-recorder since learners can dictate their ideas into the recorder, select those which meet their desired need, alter them, and finally transcribe the revised ideas. No doubt after several sessions with the tape-recorder, they should have developed the necessary skills and competencies for putting their ideas on paper.

L. *Book Review Promotion Program.* There are a number of opportunities that may be available at the secondary level for reviewing books. Often advance copies of books (such as review copies) can be obtained inexpensively by contacting publishers. Able readers may want to compose reviews for the school bulletin board or newspaper to stimulate the interest of all readers in a variety of subjects. In many cases both authors and publishers are interested in receiving copies of student reviews. Reviewers may wish to correspond directly with the author. A tele-conference may be arranged between a secondary class and the author regarding such aspects as to why he or she wrote the book, the degree of fiction material in the volume, and the areas which appeal most to students.

Special Secondary Schools and Programs for the Gifted

Research indicates that several school systems throughout the world have established schools which are especially designed for the exclusive use of students deemed to be gifted. Particular attention is given to identification, evaluation, and individualized instruction of each learner. A sampling of descriptions of several such institutions is included below.

A. *Philippine High School for The Arts* is described by Gonzalez[13] as a school for young people between the ages of 11 and 16 who are gifted in the arts and have intelligence quotients ranging to the superior levels. A reading program was constructed for these students for such purposes as to develop creative talents; assist developmental growth of the learners; increase communication skills; and help build a continuing interest in reading. To accomplish these goals, the teachers and administrators set out to (1) purchase large amounts of multilevel materials; (2) allow students to self-select books for completing assignments; and (3) encourage teachers to develop common reading skill objects in all classes. The efforts of the teachers and students produced rewarding results since English communication improved and the graduates received high scores on college entrance examinations. The program is still in use at present.

B. *California Demonstration Program in Reading.* The California State Department of Education has established a number of Demonstration Programs in Reading including one at Sierra Junior High School, 3017 Center Street, Bakersfield, California 93306. The reading and micro-management program is designed for seventh and eighth grade students and is set in a success-oriented laboratory environment for diagnostic prescriptive and reading skills building. The program provides for a wide variety of learning activities which are undertaken by learners on a contractual basis to improve competencies in such areas as comprehension, vocabulary, structural analysis, research/study skills, recreational reading, literature, and oral language. The RAM components include such aspects as the use of computers, small group instruction, motivational strategies, and team teaching techniques.

While the RAM program is utilized with all students, it is especially desirable for gifted and talented with respect to reading enrichment in the basic reading skill areas. Additionally, the self-esteem and motivation levels of students are increased substantially through the use of the program.

C. *IMPACT: A High School Gifted Program That Works.* This program involves gifted students in 24 high schools in DeKalb County, Georgia and is structured as an enrichment framework which allows students to carry on independent study in the subject area of the learner's choice.[14] They may participate in the special program at any grade level. Though there are many objectives of the program, several relate to reading and language enrichment skill proficiencies such as creative and/or scientific approaches to learning, effective and productive thinking, and activities that help them improve their abilities as innovators and problem solvers.

Each student enters into a contract with school officials to undertake a certain study which results in credits of various kinds when the project has been finished and meets the approval of a special committee consisting of the Impact teacher, student, parent, subject area teacher, and counselor. A carefully devised questionnaire study involving 358 of present and past IMPACT students resulted in the conclusion that 90 percent of the students would enroll in IMPACT if they were to repeat their high school experiences.

D. *Program For Developing Effective Study Skills and Self-Confidence.* Crittenden, Kaplan, and Heim[15] report on a research program for academically able young adolescents which was undertaken with 16 selected young people between the grades of 6–9 who had scored above average on the *Binet* and *Wechsler Scales* and group achievement tests but were underachieving. The special program consisting of seven two-hour sessions was conducted at the Language Development Clinic at the University of California Medical Center in San Francisco. During the lessons, emphasis was placed on SQ3R methods, report writing, book reports, and creative written expression. The authors concluded that the short course did appear to improve self-concept, written language, and study skills. Interestingly, the eight girls developed improved writing and study skills, but had diminished self-concepts while the eight boys seemed to gain the most from the program. Evidence from the research program appears to point to the conclusion that older students may need special instruction in such areas as lecture and text mastery while younger able students may not be intellectually ready to master abstract writing skills.

E. *Cranston's Comprehensive Reading Program.* This program is a district-wide K–12 reading instruction and management system in Cranston, Rhode Island which involves the use of such aspects as mastery criteria, instructional pacing, and parent communication and involvement. While the program is utilized for all students, gifted and talented secondary students are sure to receive motivation and build goal-setting standards since each learner is given a diagnostic instrument by the classroom teacher and the results are utilized to place each student at the appropriate instructional level. Each teacher tracks each student's progress and adjusts the pace of instruction accordingly. The system reading specialist acts as a consultant to school system personnel in developing appropriate instructional strategies. Further information may be obtained by contacting the Department of Reading Services, 50 Gladstone Street, Cranston, Rhode Island 02920.

F. *Reading Education Accountability Design: Secondary (READ:S)*. This Idaho secondary reading program is utilized with students in Grades 7–12 through teacher-developed instructional modules and/or computer-assisted lesson designs for the objective of aiding students in mastering a body of 60 sequentially listed reading skills. Emphasis is placed on such instructional strategies as direct skills instruction, reinforcement strategies, inservice programs, record-keeping management strategies, and computer-assisted components for help in managing instruction. The design should be very advantageous for gifted, superior readers since a series of tests and inventories are administered to ascertain each student's strengths as well as any limitations that may be present. Using these data, language arts and content area teachers structure the teaching curriculum to help students progress as rapidly as possible in mastering the sequence of skills which emphasize the areas of vocabulary, comprehension, and study skills. (Coeur d'Alene School District, No. 271, 311 North 10th Street, Coeur d'Alene, Idaho 83814.)

EVALUATION OF SECONDARY READING PROGRAMS FOR ABLE READERS

As noted earlier, there are a limited number of formal reading programs for gifted readers; however, there is considerable evidence that hundreds of secondary content teachers and administrators make various instructional provisions for these types of learners. This chapter contains a listing and discussion of the basic principles which should be kept in mind in developing an effective instructional program for able readers. Since in any heterogeneous school population one may find as many as 10 to 15 percent of the students in the category of gifted, it is important for educators to keep these aspects in mind and build a program of evaluation for determining the degree to which these principles have been inculcated in the total curriculum. (The total process of evaluation including purposes, principles, and formal and informal tests is discussed in Chapter VI.)

The following may serve as a form which can be utilized for estimating the degree to which a given school curriculum or program meets the need of gifted readers at the secondary level. The school official completing the form should write *yes, no* or *sometimes* on the blank previous to each statement. (In the most ideal setting, one would strive to have a "yes" response for each item.)

EVALUATION OF _____ HIGH SCHOOL
READING PROGRAM FOR GIFTED READERS

_____ 1. A program of evaluation and measurement is in place as a mechanism for collecting and analyzing data relating to the present strengths and limitations of *all* readers.

_____ 2. Provisions are made in the total curriculum for the continuous development of reading skills for superior readers in all content areas.

_____ 3. Each content teacher is aware of the present instructional and independent reading levels of able learners.

_____ 4. Special instructional programs are available for helping each superior reader reach his or her maximum level of achievement with regard to reading competency.

_____ 5. The respective roles and responsibilities of the administrator, classroom teacher, librarian, counselor, and reading specialist are thoroughly understood by all parties concerned.

_____ 6. Many advanced reading materials relating to content subject areas as well as pleasure reading are available for use by all able readers in both the classroom and library.

_____ 7. Grouping strategies are employed to allow appropriate learning experiences for those readers who have similar needs and abilities.

_____ 8. In-service teacher training programs are in evidence to provide each instructor with the skills, competencies, and abilities for constructing a classroom environment which will motivate, inspire, and cause gifted readers to realize maximum growth in such important reading skill areas as vocabulary, comprehension, study skills, and resource reading.

_____ 9. Award programs of both an intrinsic and extrinsic nature are established as a means of motivating all readers to gain a feeling of enjoyment and satisfaction as they pursue various reading assignments.

_____10. Provisions are available for the collection and utilization of student opinions and attitudes with respect to their evaluation of the reading curriculum being utilized for them.

In the space below list the three or four major strengths and limitations of our present instructional program for meeting the needs of gifted readers.

Strengths_____

_____

_____

Limitations _____

_____

_____

Based on the above information, enumerate, in order of importance, three steps administrators and teachers in this system should undertake to improve the reading instructional program for gifted readers.

1. _____

_____

2. _____

_____

3. _____

_____

The previous form may be employed with all secondary content teachers, a selected group (such as language arts faculty), or persons such as principals, department chairpersons, and individual teachers. An analysis of all data collected from the instruments may serve as a basis for forming a new reading curriculum or altering a set of existing plans.

SUMMARY

In order to construct a meaningful instructional program, educators must keep in mind the typical attitudes and characteristics of the gifted secondary reader. There are certain principles which should be remembered in shaping a useful set of reading experiences. The curriculum developed may include a special school or identifiable program for able readers or it may consist of various adaptations to an existing schedule of classes. The descriptions of existing endeavors included in this chapter may serve as an important source of information. Using the form at the close of the chapter can provide valuable indices for evaluating present endeavors.

REFERENCES

1. Anderson, Margaret A., Nona A. Tollefson, and Edwyna C. Gilbert, "Giftedness and Reading: A Cross-Sectional View of Differences in Reading Attitudes and Behaviors," *Gifted Child Quarterly,* V. 29, No. 1 (Fall, 1985) pp. 186–189.
2. Newcomer, Phyllis L. and Mary A. Goldberg, "The Relationship Between Written Expression and Reading in Gifted Adolescents," *Journal of The Education of the Gifted,* V. 5, No. 3 (Spring, 1980), pp. 91–97.
3. Swassing, Raymond H. *Teaching Gifted Children and Adolescents.* Columbus, Charles E. Merrill Publishing Company, 1985, pp. 293–294.
4. Burmeister, Lou E. *Reading Strategies For Secondary School Teachers.* Reading, Addison-Wesley Publishing Company, 1974, p. 90.
5. Greenlaw, M. Jean and David W. Moore, "What Kinds of Reading Courses are Taught in Junior and Senior High School?" *Journal of Reading,* V. 25, No. 6 (March, 1982), p. 535.
6. Gregory, Estelle H. and Judith Stevens-Long, "Coping Skills Among Highly Gifted Adolescents," *Journal For The Education of The Gifted,* V. 9, No. 2 (Winter, 1986), p. 148.
7. Kulieke, Marilynn J., "Research Design Issues in The Evaluation of Programs For The Gifted: A Case Study," *Journal For The Education of The Gifted,* V. 9, No. 3 (Spring, 1986), pp. 193–207.
8. Moller, Barbara W., "An Instructional Model for Gifted Advanced Readers," *Journal of Reading,* V. 27, No. 4 (January, 1984), pp. 324–333.
9. Brazell, Jo, "Creativity in Secondary Schools," *Creative Reading For Gifted Learners.* Newark, International Reading Association, 1974, p. 67.
10. Shepherd, David L. *Comprehensive High School Reading Methods* (Second Edition). Columbus, Charles E. Merrill Publishing Company, 1978, p. 175.
11. Cagney, Margaret A. and Elizabeth H. Sakiey, "Enrichment Activities For the Gifted Reader," *Reading Improvement,* V. 21, No. 3 (Fall, 1984), p. 166.
12. Swassing, op. cit., p. 303.
13. Gonzalez, Esperanza A., "A Reading Program for The Gifted in The Philippines," *Journal of Reading,* V. 24, No. 8 (May, 1981), pp. 707–711.
14. Dubner, Frances S., "IMPACT: A High School Gifted Program That Works," *Roeper Review,* V. 7, No. 1 (September, 1984), pp. 41–43.
15. Crittenden, Mary R., Marjorie H. Kaplan, and Judith K. Heim, "Developing Effective Study Skills and Self-Confidence in Academically Able Young Adolescents," *Gifted Child Quarterly,* V. 28, No. 1 (Winter, 1984), pp. 25–30.

CHAPTER VI

EVALUATING READING SKILLS OF
GIFTED AND TALENTED LEARNERS

The process of evaluation is an important segment of the teaching-learning curriculum of gifted and talented learners since the data derived from various formal and informal strategies serve as the basis for constructing a meaningful, individualized program of reading instruction which meets the personal needs of the learner. The evaluation procedures provide the instructor with valuable information relating to such matters as strengths and limitations in the important reading skill areas and present instructional reading grade level.

Evaluation constitutes at least two of the steps involved in the construction and implementation of an effective reading program for gifted and able learners. *First,* the skills and competencies that should be mastered should be determined; *second,* a program of evaluation must be undertaken to determine the degree to which individual students have accomplished skill mastery; *third,* an instructional procedures curriculum must be established to help pupils learn the desired skills at a maximum rate; and *fourth,* further evaluation must be undertaken to determine the extent of proficiency realized by the instructional program.

In planning a program of reading skill development for gifted and talented students, a very careful analysis must be undertaken to determine his or her present reading abilities in order to build a practical reading program that will help the pupil reach his or her potential or capacity reading level. These procedures may include the use of diagnostic-prescriptive teaching methods which are employed on an individual basis to the degree that staff and resources permit.

This chapter is concerned with a number of topics which provide valuable information relative to the total process of evaluation and how it relates to building an effective reading program for gifted learners. The following aspects are discussed: the nature of evaluation; purposes of evaluation; principles of an effective program of evaluation; standardized and informal reading tests; and utilizing the results of reading

101

evaluation instruments. A summary and a list of references utilized in the material are included at the close of the chapter.

THE NATURE OF EVALUATION

The total reading curriculum for any student should be constructed on the basis of his or her present strengths and limitations with the view of promoting those instructional strategies which will result in maximizing learning at the highest possible level. The structuring of a comprehensive evaluation sequence is a challenging task since it demands many teaching competencies. Among other aspects, he or she needs to have a broad acquaintance of the types of commercial and informal tests which are available, the purposes of the various instruments, and the scoring and interpretation principles involved with each tool. Perhaps the most important of all teacher competencies is that of utilizing evaluative test data to compose effective, individualized reading instruction for all pupils, especially those who are gifted and talented.

The history of measurement and evaluation has been long and interesting. As far back as 2200 B.C., the Chinese administered essay examinations to various students. Much later, famous educators such as Socrates, Campbell, and Horace Mann developed oral and written examinations. Thorndike, Binet, Otis, and Cattell developed various intelligence tests in the late 1800's and early 1900's.[1] Many and varied achievement tests have been written and normed during the past fifty years. The results of both intelligence and achievement tests have been regularly utilized by educators for the purposes of placement, grading, and general measurement.

At the present time, it is important to draw a distinction between **evaluation** and **measurement**. Gronlund[2] notes that from an instructional standpoint, **evaluation** may be defined as a **systematic process of determining the extent to which instructional objectives are achieved by pupils.** He notes that **measurement** is limited to the quantitative descriptions of pupils (number correct out of 100 on a reading test) while **evaluation** is a much more comprehensive and inclusive term and may include quantitative *and* qualitative descriptions of pupils, or both, and always include value judgments of the teacher.

A further explanation of the differences between measurement and evaluation is offered by Mehrens and Lehmann[3] who indicate that two students may obtain the same test score, but we might evaluate those measures differently. For example, two fifth grade students may be reading at the fifth grade level at the end of the school year; however, at the beginning of the year, one student was reading at the third grade level and one at the fourth grade, fifth month level. It is obvious that one learner read at a below average rate and the other at an above average rate.

It is the goal of measurement to take the irregular behaviors of humans and quantify them. Further, it is the central dogma of measurement that words used to describe the traits and characteristics of humans can be expressed as numbers; however, this is not an easy process.[4] The total process of evaluation involves a number of complex items and the mere administration and scoring of a teacher-constructed or commercial reading test cannot possibly reveal all of the profound strengths and limitations of any given learner. The placement and ongoing instruction in reading for gifted and talented readers requires educators to make the distinction between mere measurement and more comprehensive evaluative procedures. The purposes of evaluation must be thoroughly understood and integrated in a well-constructed program of reading instruction. Data derived from various evaluative instruments and strategies can be a significant source of information for developing objectives and preparing lessons and techniques that meet the precise instructional needs of the gifted learner.

THE PURPOSES OF EVALUATION

The first major purpose of evaluation is to help teachers formulate appropriate teaching objectives for the able reader. Walter Hill[5] believes that effective reading evaluation should help to develop precise, realistic ultimate and immediate objectives for the total reading program and classroom reading instruction by determining the current reading needs of pupils and monitoring the usefulness of present objectives. Since there are many diverse skill aspects of the reading process, one must establish future individual, instructional goals based on the gifted pupil's present level of competency in such areas as word attack, comprehension, vocabulary, study skills, and reading rate. One of the major errors committed by educators is to assume that most, if not all, students have similar needs and thus a common set of objectives and lesson plans can be used appropriately with all learners, including those who have demonstrated advanced reading skills. Repeated demands by teachers for

able pupils to complete simplistic homework assignments may possibly
lead to boredom, frustration, and anti-social behavior. Though it demands
much planning and organization, the instructional goals of gifted pupils
must be constructed apart from those which are designed for the total
class.

Many new reading tests that have pencil and paper and computer
applications provide an in-depth assessment and detailed error analysis
for each learner. One such test is the *Kaufman Test of Educational Achievement* (American Guidance Service) which was first marketed in 1985.
This individually administered achievement test yields comparable data
on math, reading, and spelling and can be used for continuous assessment from Grades 1 through 12. The examiner can undertake a clinical
analysis of the data and use the information to plan both short-term and
interim instructional objectives and strategies. Other uses include the
ability to formulate hypotheses about a student's test performance, his/her
relative strengths, and applicable learning strategies which may be applied.
The instrument supplies a variety of scores including stanines, age and
grade equivalents, as well as standard scores. One valuable piece of
research information for the gifted educator is the provision of correlation studies which have been recently conducted between the Brief Form
and the *WRAT, PIAT, K-ABC,* and the *PPVT-R* instruments.

**Evaluation procedures should provide valuable information for educators in
helping them discover which learning style is preferred by the individual gifted
reader.** All readers, especially those who are gifted, read with enthusiasm
and confidence when they are taught by methods which recognize their
preferred learning style. Knowing this information can be of much
assistance in helping the teacher build an individualized, tailor-made,
effective reading procedure to employ with each learner. This plan will
help the learner by increasing the level of pleasurable reading, improving attitude, and maximizing reading achievement performance.

There are numerous, efficient ways of classifying the preferred learning style of each student through the use of careful observation, student-
teacher dialogue, and the use of various informal strategies such as the
cloze test, informal reading inventory, and commercial instruments such
as the *Frostig Developmental Test of Visual Perception* (Publishers Test
Service) and the *Wepman Auditory Discrimination Test* (Western Psychological Services).

A new instrument entitled *Reading Style Inventory* (Learning Research
Associates, Inc.) identifies each student's best way to read through a

computer analyzed procedure which suggests the best method to reach each student. This diagnostic tool is unique since it clarifies a student's learning style for reading and recommends the specific strategies, materials, and methods that each learner needs to read most effectively. The R.S.I. instrument can be administered by using either the classroom computer or test booklets and answer sheets. It can be administered individually or in a group setting for students in Grades 2 through 12 and requires approximately 15 to 30 minutes testing time. Scoring can be undertaken through the use of the school computer printer or the answer sheets can be sent to the publisher for processing. The process sheet contains valuable information for the teacher relating to such individual areas as perceptual strengths/preferences, preferred reading environment, emotional profile, sociological preferences, and physical preferences. R.S.I. group profiles can also be formulated which list students alphabetically and divide them into appropriate reading style groups, indicate reading style strengths and preferences for each student, and contain group totals for all reading styles categories. These data should prove to be extremely valuable for designing a reading program which would be highly motivating and challenging for the able reader at any grade level.

A significant role of an effective evaluation program is to provide valuable information to help teachers and administrators in the process of grouping students who are gifted readers that will result in maximum reading achievement for each learner. There are numerous types of procedures that may be used such as interclass and intraclass grouping to attain a satisfactory learning environment. There is some indication that general homogeneous grouping is inclined to be advantageous for high ability pupils in increasing their achievement. At the same time, the segregation by mental or reading ability or both reduces the competition present in groups of mixed ability.[6] In order to make a proper decision about the membership of the groups, the teacher must make a careful study of each learner's evaluative data including achievement test data, informal test information, and anecdotal statements of previous teachers. With any type of grouping method, instructors must remember to keep the membership of groups flexible enough to allow those students who make significant progress to join the next more advanced class.

The length of time for gathering pertinent data for the purpose of grouping learners may involve a period of several weeks duration. Two authorities[7] note that during this period of time, teachers should listen to their students read orally, observe their ability to answer questions about material they have read silently, and note how they interact socially. These kinds of information should be of much help in discovering which students have similar instructional and independent reading levels. At this point the able readers can be identified and appropriate materials and teaching strategies can be selected.

A carefully devised evaluation program can yield important data for determining the degree and level of reading achievement obtained by gifted readers both individually and collectively in the three learning domains. Even among very able learners, a significant degree of difference may exist among and between learners with respect to skill proficiencies in the three basic learning domains. In the **affective domain,** for example, two very capable pupils who have very impressive instructional reading skill levels may have widely varying feelings and attitudes with regard to viewing reading as a pleasurable activity. The feelings which a given young person may have had a significant influence on his or her eagerness to pursue regular classroom reading assignments and recreational reading activities.

In the **perceptual domain,** perception can be defined as giving meaning to sensations or the ability to organize stimuli on a field. How readers organize stimuli depends on their background of experience and the various sensory receptors.[8] Usually, gifted readers perform satisfactorily in the perceptual area; however, a small percentage of learners who may possess various neurological handicaps and dyslexic symptoms may exhibit some perceptual deficiencies. For example, a few highly gifted readers may write letters and words which are so profoundly illegible that teachers and others cannot read and comprehend their written essays. It is important to remember that perception skills are dependent upon a variety of factors including motivation, attention span, word meaning skills, and psychological closure. Those readers who have pronounced deficiencies should be given individual instruction in the areas of weakness.

The **cognitive domain** is involved with thinking and processing, transforming, and remembering information. A careful item analysis by either computer or pencil and paper methods of achievement test results can be of tremendous value in determining the degree to which an able reader is proficient in the total areas of vocabulary and comprehension. Those who have limitations may need to be grouped for further instruction.

Evaluative strategies may produce useful data for making important decisions regarding the precise kinds and types of instructional materials needed by gifted readers. As suggested by the appendices section of this volume, there is a wide variety of print media and computer software which is available for reading instruction of all pupils, especially those who are highly proficient learners. A careful analysis of both formal and informal evaluative strategies should lend invaluable clues to the teacher regarding the most satisfactory teaching tools to purchase. The microcomputer may be exceptionally useful since it allows the learner to spend a considerable amount of time on task, provides immediate feedback to the student relating to his or her progress, awards the participant through a series of innovative graphics, and serves as a diagnostic, prescriptive, and teaching tool for steady reading skill development. Practically all gifted and talented pupils respond well to computer programs when appropriate software has been selected by school officials. Due to the fact that there are dozens of companies engaged in software production, the proper selection of software should be based on such aspects as the instructional and independent reading levels of the learners, the basic purpose of the tools, cost, and ease of use.

The purchase of computer software for all pupils, especially able learners, should be undertaken with the utmost care and attention. Zealous marketing agents tout many advantages of computer programs including drill and practice, tutorial programs, teaching games, and discovering proper reading level of the learner. However, Eugene Jongsma[9] warns that reading teachers should be cognizant of various limitations and restraints imposed by some software manufacturers such as not allowing customers to preview programs before they are purchased, the inability to return unsatisfactory products, and the payment of expenses involved. These aspects should lead all buyers to be especially wary when purchasing software.

A significant purpose of a well-devised program of reading evaluation is to provide pertinent data for the teacher, counselor, and administrator for establishing a cooperative plan of future studies for the learner. As the student moves upward from one grade or learning level to the next, the able reader needs to be enrolled in those programs and courses of study which are most helpful and accommodating to his or her instructional needs. The proper identification of gifted students lends important data that may serve as a basis for planning future curricula for the students. The need for employing additional educational specialists may be established along with the construction of unique programs such as those described in the previous chapter. When building these programs, educators need to utilize other persons when studying a large body of evaluative data. The plan should make use of the collective judgment of the class-room teacher, counselor, principal, gifted coordinator, public officials, and parents of able readers when their input would be useful.

A final goal of evaluation is to provide a bank of vital data for completing important school studies about the present and future reading programs for the gifted in a given school system. At the present time many states provide special funding for those pupils who have been identified as gifted. Those monies, supplemented by local school budgets, allow local school officials to employ special teachers and coordinators for the gifted. Precise information relating to a variety of aspects must be provided such as (a) criteria used for identifying gifted pupils; (b) number of designated learners at each grade level; (c) objectives of the curriculum such as reading and other skill areas; and (d) methods by which the program and skill progression of individual students will be evaluated. Computerized procedures may be employed for storing achievement test results which describe the year-by-year growth of gifted pupils in such important areas as vocabulary, comprehension, study skills, and rate of reading. Assuming that a steady progression of achievement has taken place, these data may serve as a basis for requests for further funding of future programs in individual schools within a district as well as for the total school district.

In *summary*, a well-devised program of reading evaluation serves a number of purposes including formulating suitable teaching objectives, identifying preferred learning styles, grouping learners for maximum achievement, assessing the degree and level of reading achievement of gifted readers, providing the proper teaching materials for able students, and establishing a storehouse of valuable data for use in planning future learning programs.

PRINCIPLES OF AN EFFECTIVE PROGRAM OF EVALUATION

If the purposes of evaluation are to be effectively realized and made a part of a vibrant curriculum for gifted readers, there must be a body of well-defined principles which are involved at every stage of program development. The continual diagnosis of both pupils' reading develop-ment and teachers' reading instruction is a major feature of effective teaching of reading. Ongoing diagnosis in these two basic areas forms the foundation for planning reading instruction and determining its effectiveness.[10]

A broad approach to evaluation should be taken, especially when undertaking a program of diagnosis. If we see reading as a total integrative process, diagnosis should also be seen as a total integrative process. Numerous aspects should be considered including personal, environmental, intellectual, educative, and noneducative factors.[11]

As the reading evaluation program is developed, there are several strategic principles which should be considered. If these are given priority during the construction process, the amount of positive help for both teachers and pupils will be enlarge. The following are ten important guidelines to remember. They are not listed in any particular order of importance, thus each should receive roughly equal attention.

1. **The most important product to be derived from any effective program of evaluation is that of improving instruction for all pupils, especially gifted readers.** Unfortunately, in some situations data derived from achievement and other tests are recorded on a pupil's office records and little use is made of the information for improving instructional modes for the learner. Teachers of all children should make a careful analysis of the test results since it may reveal that the present method of instruction is not resulting in the kind of growth that one may expect for a given pupil. For example, one may wish to make a comparison between the child's present achievement level and the reading expectancy level which may result from the application of the Bond and Tinker formula.[12] As researchers assume that the I.Q. is, in one respect, an index of rate of learning, we can estimate the reading potential of each child by means of the **reading expectancy** formula:

$$\frac{\text{I.Q.}}{100} \times \text{years of reading instruction} + 1.0 = \frac{\text{reading}}{\text{expectancy}}$$

An able learner with an I.Q. of 150 at the beginning of the fourth grade should be reading at the 5.5 level (1.50 times 3 + 1).

Results from diagnostic tests such as the *Durrell Analysis of Reading Difficulty, New Edition (1980)* (Harcourt Brace Jovanovich, Inc.) and the *Woodcock Reading Mastery Test* (American Guidance Service) may be utilized to define clearly the type of reading instruction which is most valid for a particular student. When revising instructional patterns, a global analysis should be taken of a body of test data rather than complete attention given to a single score.

2. **Evaluation procedures should be undertaken on both a periodic and continuous basis.** To secure the most current assessment of a given pupil's

ability in reading requires daily informal assessment of his or her performance in such areas as vocabulary, comprehension, and word attack through the use of observational techniques, cloze procedures, and subjective reading inventories. Lessons need to be constructed that are based on **current** abilities and not on what data may have been collected from an achievement test administered several months previous. As noted earlier, each learner has a preferred learning style and level of potential and these aspects must be utilized in altering daily lesson plans that are most useful and applicable for any particular day. Daily interaction with all able readers through meaningful daily assignments should enable the teacher to construct lesson plans which are designed to meet individual needs and help maximize success in building all of the major skill areas. Since parent-teacher conferences may yield important anecdotal information, careful attention should be given to parent comments and reactions that may lend insights relating to pupil attitudes and feelings. Sharing examples of **daily** work are helpful in explaining a pupil's academic progress during the parent-teacher conference. The study of diagnostic and achievement test data along with an evaluation of daily work can serve as a valuable basis for planning both current and future reading lessons for the able student. A computerized item analysis of achievement test results can lend valuable help in constructing unit lessons that will help the learner to improve skill development in areas of limitation. Meaningful comparisons can be made between standardized test results and skill proficiencies demonstrated on daily work assignments.

3. **The evaluation process should be conducted with a broad perspective in mind.** As noted earlier, there is a distinct difference between *measurement* and *evaluation.* Measurement is concerned chiefly with a specific score on a given commercial or teacher-made test, whereas evaluation takes into account many different aspects such as commercial tests, informal instruments, and impressions received from conversations and observation of pupils, both individually and collectively. For example, Lapp and Flood[13] believe that the teacher should consider several points when undertaking reading diagnosis. These include the strengths and needs of the students, role of diagnostic evaluation in the classroom, knowledge brought by the students to a specific topic, and the skills needed to pursue the study of this topic.

In some instances, teachers have a tendency to place undue reliance on standardized achievement test results believing that they are somewhat precise in their evaluation of reading ability. One must remember that standardized achievement tests were designed, as their test makers state, to measure the achievement of **groups** of individuals. Standardized achievement scales tell us something about groups. They do not tell us anything about individuals. Teachers and parents must not expect these scores to be accurate for individuals.[14]

In light of the inherent limitations of all kinds of instruments, the teacher needs to consider a total range of scores obtained from a variety of sources. Cognitive skill development may be primarily measured through commercial and teacher-made tests whereas affective domain aspects need the careful observation of the teacher for positive assessment. The verbal and non-verbal cues given by the learner should also prove to be important indices in conducting a global estimate of his or her present level of reading accomplishment.

4. **The purposes of the administration of various evaluation instruments and strategies should be explained to the person being evaluated.** The cooperation of the student should be sought at every stage of the evaluation process since pupils are an integral part of the process of assessment and optimum performance can only be expected when the student understands that the results will be utilized for program improvement and not as a basis for issuing inferior grades or marks. A few gifted readers may actually develop the unfortunate impression that it **may not be** helpful to perform at the maximum level since the teacher may assign more lessons to him or her. Thus, the attitude with which a student approaches an evaluative experience is highly critical to the level and kind of response accorded by the learner. If students understand that all evaluation strategies are designed solely to benefit their personal reading abilities, they will be more agreeable with regard to exhibiting their best efforts when responding to test items.

5. **The administration of classroom tests of both a commercial and teacher-made variety, should be undertaken with the premise that each and every student will have a fair and equal opportunity to demonstrate his or her current level of achievement in light of the teaching skill objectives being tested.** Good test administration requires that a number of principles be followed.

   a. **The level of test anxiety of students has a clear relationship to the type of performance demonstrated on the test.** It is best to avoid such comments as (a) warning pupils that they may fail the course if they do poorly on this test, (b) they must work quickly to finish the test, and

(c) school privileges may be removed if they fail the examination. The timing of the test is important, thus important tests should not be scheduled the afternoon of the homecoming party or pep assembly for the grudge football game of the season.

b. **Directions for the test should be given as clearly as possible with assorted, unrelated comments kept to a minimum.** Since most, if not all, standardized tests are timed examinations, learners feel they have been shortchanged if they are not given the entire allowable time period to complete the examination. Comments relating to the next unit, the speaker for next Wednesday's class, or the dates of the upcoming two unit tests are distracting and superfluous and build unnecessary stress for the learners.

c. **Keep distractions to a minimum during the time a test is administered.** It is best to post a "do not disturb" sign on the door and advise the school secretary to avoid making announcements on the school sound system. Proofread the test carefully and ask learners to make appropriate corrections on the test **before** the test actually begins. Intermittent requests for students to change wording or correct a typographical error adds greatly to test anxiety.

d. **Utilize procedures to eliminate the copying of answers or other cheating strategies.** The vast majority of students are honest; however, for the small number who are dishonest, several actions on the part of the teacher can discourage such practices. **First,** establish special seating arrangements by leaving every other seat vacant or moving desks a sufficient distance from each other and thus making it very difficult for one student to see a classmate's paper. **Second,** move about the room quietly to let the pupils know that the instructor is carefully monitoring their work. **Third,** be sure to collect carefully all test booklets and answer sheets at the close of the testing period.

6. **The instructor should render an evaluation of an able reader's level of reading skill development only after a study of a pattern of scores from several testing strategies has been made.** For example, if one is to establish the approximate instructional reading of a pupil, the results from both a standardized achievement test and informal techniques should be analyzed. The learner in question may not function satisfactorily on one instrument because of physical problems, emotional distress, or general lack of motivation. To discover the proficiency level of a student in the area of comprehension, one may need to study the percentile and stanine scores from the comprehension section of the commercial achievement test; information secured from a series of teacher-constructed comprehension tests; and the evaluation of how well the pupil responds to oral comprehension questions asked by the teacher during class discussions. Due to

the fact that all evaluation strategies have varying levels of validity and reliability, the careful inspection of a total pattern of scores is both useful and imperative.

7. **Before selecting any type of commercial instrument, one needs to consult reliable sources for information about the advantages and possible limitations which may be attendant concerning a given test.** There are several authoritative sources such as *Mental Measurements Yearbook, Tests in Print,* and *Reading Tests and Reviews* which contain valuable information regarding practically all nationally distributed commercial intelligence and reading tests. (These three volumes are available from the University of Nebraska Press, 901 North 17th Street, Lincoln, Nebraska 68586). Additional opinions may be secured from fellow classroom teachers and administrators who have purchased and administered various tests. These data can be of immense value in establishing the face validity of such instruments. The prospect of computerized scoring with individual item analyses is a valuable consideration when making a test selection. The degree of internal correlation between skill objectives of the reading program and the nature of the test items should be studied carefully. Other aspects such as validity, reliability, and standard error of measurement should be evaluated and made part of the final consideration.

8. **The evaluation program should involve the use of a wide range of commercial and teacher-constructed testing devices.** Every testing instrument has inherent strengths and limitations and cannot possibly be comprehensive in evaluating all aspects of the reading act. For example, standardized achievement tests in reading are designed primarily to measure a given learner's ability in the cognitive skill areas of comprehension and vocabulary but have very limited use for measuring affective domain segments such as love of reading and interest in various types of literature. To gain information relating to a pupil's feelings and impressions about reading requires the use of structured interviews and the completion of reading interest inventories. Informal devices such as cloze procedures and subjective inventories are not standardized and thus statistical comparisons cannot be made through the use of stanines, percentiles, and grade placement scores. To assess adequately all phases of reading skill development requires a meaningful mixture of numerous devices with the understanding that each has advantages and limitations for evaluation purposes. The results obtained from a composite group of instruments can be helpful in planning a well-defined program

of reading instruction for any learner, especially one who is gifted and talented.

9. A precise and careful recording of all evaluation data should be maintained for each student. This objective could be accomplished through the use of noting all information on cumulative record folders or through the use of computer software which contains a current record of past and present evaluation scores that can be noted on a viewing screen by merely indicating a pupil's name and/or identification number. As noted earlier, there are instruments such as the *Reading Style Inventory* which allow for computerized print sheets which can be separated and placed in a student's cumulative folder. Some software programs will allow the computer printer to record the names of all students who received a test score above or below a critical score level which was determined earlier by the instructor.

10. Finally, increasing emphasis should be placed on self-appraisal as the student grows older. Unless a pupil develops a personal understanding of his or her reading strengths and limitations, the results noted from a nationally published test may not be very meaningful. There are numerous avenues available for teachers to utilize self-appraisal techniques. Some of these are:

1. Asking the student to proofread a paper written recently to try to discover errors in grammar and spelling.
2. Inviting the learner to listen to a tape-recording of a classroom speech or discussion in which he or she participated and strive to detect mispronounced words and grammar errors. Perhaps volume and pitch can also be noted as areas where improvement may be made.

Following each of these activities, invite the learner to write a list of reading, writing, or listening skills which may be improved. Beside each skill note a critical score which is sought along with an approximate date when it is hoped the competency will be attained. If there is proper classroom rapport, the teacher may desire to have certain learners exchange papers and attempt to locate predetermined limitations in areas such as incorrect grammar or misspelled words. By noting the strengths and limitations of peers, a learner may gain the correct impression regarding the kinds and types of errors he or she should try to avoid. As noted in this section, there are numerous principles of an effective evaluation program which should be observed by all teachers of all types of readers, especially those who are gifted and talented. These include the improvement of instruction, long-range planning and administration of evaluation measures, development of a broad perspective, careful administration of tests, study of a broad range of scores, and increasing emphasis on self-analysis of reading skill strengths and limitations.

STANDARDIZED AND INFORMAL READING TESTS

There are large numbers of standardized and informal reading tests available to teachers and administrators for the purpose of conducting a continuous assessment of the different reading strengths of individuals as well as groups of pupils. In order to build an instructional program that takes into account the various needs of individual learners requires the teacher to have a wide variety of evaluation tools and strategies for immediate and long-range use. Teachers should use a combination of teacher observation, formal tests, and informal tests to assemble the materials needed to begin a diagnostic-prescriptive program. The final goal is to use the data obtained from assessment to construct an effective, well-managed diagnostic-prescriptive reading program which will meet the needs of the individual student.[15]

To apprise the present reading achievement levels of able learners requires the use of such tools as informal or subjective reading inventories, pupil placement tests, teacher-made instruments, criterion-referenced tests, and standardized norm-referenced tests. Within the general group of standardized instruments one can find norm-referenced, criterion-referenced, and diagnostic reading tests. In the sections which follow, a description of some of the more commonly utilized standardized and informal tests are given along with brief references relating to their special applications for gifted readers.

Standardized Reading Tests

With regard to standardized tests, there are two general types: norm-referenced and criterion-referenced tests. As compared with informal tests, standardized achievement tests have certain rather unique features which set them apart from other kinds of tools. Gronlund[16] notes that test items are of high technical quality, possess standard administration and scoring procedures, contain norms which are based on various age and grade groups, provide equivalent forms, and present a test manual as a guide for administering, scoring, and interpreting the results of the test.

There are numerous **norm-referenced** tests in the area of reading achievement for making a comparison of a given pupil's score with those scores obtained from other students who participated in the local, state, and national norming groups. Using either pencil and paper or computerized methods, it is possible to convert a learner's raw score to such indices as a stanine, percentile rank, and grade-level equivalent. With regard to those pupils who may be considered gifted readers, school officials may generally expect the following performances to be typical.

Stanines. Since stanines represent a range of scores from a low of 1 to a high of 9, the typical able reader should normally demonstrate a score representative of the 8th or 9th stanine when one considers his or her test performance over the entire range of subtests (such as vocabulary, comprehension, and word attack) that are found on the instrument.

Percentile Rank. This designation is for an indication of the percentage of students in a norming group which scored above and below a particular pupil's score. Normally, one would expect the majority of pupils who are especially gifted to score in the 90th to the 99th percentile. Some reading educators are of the opinion that the percentile rank score may be the most valid of all test result aspects.

Grade-Level Equivalent. This title represents the performance of a student on a standardized test in comparison to the average score for a designated grade level of the local, state, or national norm groups. For example, if Susan (who is a third grader) has a grade-level equivalent of 5.2, one can determine her raw score on the test was equal to the average pupil in the norming group who was in the second month of school in the fifth grade. It is important to remember that the **sizes** of learning which constitutes Grade 1, or 4, or 8 are not necessarily equal units. Zintz and Maggart[17] warn that teachers need also to recognize that while achievement at 5.0 means beginning fifth grade for **fifth** graders, achievement of an 8.0 on a test for fifth graders means they are achieving extremely well, but they may not be able to perform as beginning eighth graders.

Many gifted readers demonstrate grade-level equivalent scores which may be two to four grade levels in excess of their actual grade level placements. These data should be used in a global manner along with information derived from other standardized tests and informal instruments. Undertaking an item analysis study of all items on a standardized test through the use of computerized sheets will help to determine those exact skill areas which need further reinforcement.

Criterion-referenced tests are an important segment of the standardized test market. These examinations don't compare a given pupil's score with some other learner in the norming group but merely note the learner's level of behavioral skill achievement on an item such as "pupil can alphabetize in order a list of ten words in scrambled order." In the case of a nationally recognized test, the test author establishes a criteria of correctness for each test section. For example, the test authors may determine that a pupil has mastered the preceding behavior skill if he or she alphabetizes at least eight of the ten items correctly. Those students who score less than 8 are in need of further teaching and reinforcement with regard to this skill.

There are certain aspects of both norm-referenced and criterion-referenced tests that should be carefully considered by teachers as they utilize them with their gifted readers. The administrator's manual should be read carefully with particular attention given to the objectives of the test, administration and scoring procedures, and the important data relating to such vital segments as the validity, reliability, and standard error of measurement. The use of computer printers for analyzing special types of information is of unique use for teachers. Data available include grouping of pupils by grade level equivalents, completing item analysis surveys noting the skill strengths and limitations of individual students and as a part of a group statistical picture.

Some tests can yield precise analyses relating to preferred learning style (*Reading Style Inventory,* Learning Research Associates) and skill levels (*Stanford Diagnostic Reading Test,* Harcourt Brace Jovanovich, Inc.).

Group Standardized Reading Achievement Tests

There are numerous group standardized reading achievement tests which can be utilized very profitably for assessing current levels of reading proficiency in many skill areas such as vocabulary, comprehension, word attack, listening comprehension, and study skills. As noted earlier, there are several objective sources which can be consulted regarding such important aspects as validity, reliability, and general usability. *Tests in Print, Reading Tests and Reviews, Mental Measurement Yearbook,* and the *Test Review* section of *The Reading Teacher* (International Reading Association) all contain valuable information about tests. Other factors to be considered include age and grade level of students, objectives of the reading program, and computer applications with regard to scoring and instructional recommendations.

The following nationally recognized achievement tests are utilized by many school systems and possess very acceptable validity and reliability levels.

1. *California Achievement Test* (California Test Bureau/McGraw Hill) has five different subtests intended for lower primary through the secondary school levels and assesses such skill areas as vocabulary, comprehension, language, listening, and spelling.

2. *Gates-MacGinitie Reading Tests* (Riverside Publishing Company) measures vocabulary, comprehension, speed, and accuracy. There are five levels with separate tests for Grades 1, 2, 3, 4–6, 7–9, and 10–12.

3. *Iowa Tests of Basic Skills* (Houghton-Mifflin Company) has three alternate forms and is suitable for pupils from Grades 3 through 9. Each test is timed and measures the important skill areas of vocabulary, comprehension, language skills, and work-study skills. This instrument is carefully normed with national and regional student groups on a regular basis. Company assessment of class answer data is available and provides valuable information relating to item analysis, grade equivalents, and other data can be included.

4. *Metropolitan Reading Instructional Tests* (Harcourt Brace Jovanovich, Inc.) are available in two forms and produce results based on both norm-referenced and criterion-referenced data. An analysis of test performance can result in gaining an estimate of the instructional reading level of the pupil. There are six separate tests which may be employed for pupils from kindergarten through the ninth grade levels and provide valuable performance data relating to such skills as auditory discrimination, vocabulary in context, word part clues, rate of comprehension, and skimming and scanning.

5. *Nelson Reading Skills Test* (Riverside Publishing Company) has three levels for Grades 3.0–4.5; 4.6–6.9; and 7.0–9.9 and measures a pupil's proficiency in the areas of vocabulary and comprehension with optional tests available for word parts and rate tests. The basic test relating to vocabulary and comprehension requires thirty minutes for administration.

6. *S.R.A. Survey of Basic Skills* (Science Research Associates, Inc.) is a battery of materials consisting of eight levels that can be employed from the kindergarten through twelfth grade levels and measures such skill

components as vocabulary, comprehension, auditory discrimination, and decoding.

7. *Stanford Achievement Tests* (Harcourt Brace Jovanovich, Inc.) are designed for Grades 1–9 and contain numerous subtests in such areas as comprehension, vocabulary, paragraph meaning, spelling, and language. The Advanced Battery for Grades 7–9 is especially useful for assessing proficiency in paragraph meaning.

In addition to the seven group tests just described, other achievement instruments that may be employed include the *Diagnostic Reading Tests* (Committee on Diagnostic Testing); *Metropolitan Reading Tests* (*Psychological*); and the *Nelson-Denny Reading Test* (Riverside).

Individual Standardized Reading Tests

Though individualized instruments are used more frequently with average and disabled readers, they can serve a valuable function when used with gifted and talented readers in determining the precise reading skills which should be reinforced. For example, a few able readers are ineffective spellers and have difficulty with functional reading skills. The global assessment of a body of test data can help the instructor of the gifted to tailor an individualized program of instruction which will help the reader to become completely proficient in all aspects of reading. The following individualized tests are utilized by many reading specialists for all types of readers.

1. *Diagnostic Reading Scales* (1981 Edition) (Publishers Test Service) can be used with pupils from Grades 1 through 8. The DRS-81 test yields data relating to the nature and extent of oral reading errors, decoding skills proficiency and approximate instructional reading level.

2. *Durrell Analysis of Reading Difficulty* (1980) (Harcourt Brace Jovanovich, Inc.) is intended for Grades 1–6 and evaluates a variety of reading skill areas including oral and silent reading, spelling, handwriting, and visual memory of words.

3. *Gates-McKillop-Horowitz Reading Diagnostic Tests* (1981) (Teachers College Press) measures efficiency of oral reading, recognition of whole words, auditory blending, spelling, and oral vocabulary.

4. *New Macmillan Reading Analysis* (1985) (Macmillan Education Ltd.) is an individually administered oral reading test suitable for pupils who are 7 to 9 years of age. Among the purposes for the test is to diagnose reading achievement in the primary grades. The test was developed and

standardized in London and standardized on 600 children of average reading ability. If the NMRA is adopted in a school system, one individual should be responsible for administering it.[18]

5. *Peabody Individual Achievement Test* (PIAT) (American Guidance Service) is an individually administered instrument which is useful for measuring word recognition and reading comprehension skills for persons from the kindergarten through adult levels.

6. *Reading Style Inventory* (Learning Research Associates, Inc.) may be used either in group or individual situations and supplies data relating to each student's preferred learning style, provides tailor-made effective methods to use with each student, and recommends specific reading materials to use with each learner.

7. *Skills Monitoring System-Reading* (Harcourt Brace Jovanovich, Inc.) is a criterion-referenced tool which may be used either individually or in a group. The Blue, Green, and Purple levels are intended for Grades 3 through 5 and measure the degree of skill proficiency in word identification and comprehension.

8. *Spendafore Diagnostic Reading Test* (Publishers Test Service) can be employed with a wide range of individuals from Grade 1 through the adult levels. The criterion-referenced tool assesses comprehension in three contexts: oral reading, silent reading, and listening comprehension. Test performance can be evaluated in terms of independent, instructional, and frustration reading and comprehension levels.

9. *Wide Range Achievement Test* (1984) (Publishers Test Service) can be used in either individual or group situations and helps to establish the coding ability in reading, spelling and arithmetic. The latest edition provides derived scores and grade estimates by age for ages 5 through 11 for Level 1 and 12 through 75 for Level 2. Administration takes 15 to 30 minutes and can be hand scored in less than five minutes.

10. *Woodcock Reading Mastery Test* (American Guidance Service) is a criterion-referenced test which is available in two forms and can be utilized with all students from Grades 1–12. Various subtests involve letter and word identification, word comprehension, and passage comprehension. Information can be derived relating to such aspects as easy reading level, reading grade score, and failure reading level for each subtest.

Other commercial individual reading tests include the *Classroom Reading Inventory* (William C. Brown); *Diagnostic Reading Inventory* (Kendall Hunt); *Gilmore Oral Reading Tests* (Psychological Corporation); *Gray Oral*

Reading Tests (Psychological Corporation); and *Roswell-Chall Diagnostic Reading Test of Word Recognition Skills* (Essay).

Informal Reading Tests

As indicated earlier, it is important to attain assessment from a broad based approach that involves both standardized and informal measures. The strategies described in the following section are classroom-tested, easily compiled, and can be functional in many individual and classwide settings. Data can be gained from the instruments which will help the teacher to group pupils, utilize the proper book with a given reader, and help gifted readers increase proficiency in the basic reading skill areas. Individual tests should be given generally to those able readers who are reading at below expected levels but have a potential for reading at or above grade level. The directions for constructing and administering the test should be followed carefully to facilitate maximum validity and reliability levels and be most useful for designing ideal instructional programs.

Sight Word Vocabulary Test

One important aspect of reading is the degree of vocabulary skill possessed by that gifted reader. The following inventory is designed to provide information to sight word vocabulary proficiency.

The initial step in building the inventory is to find materials that are written at several grade levels. A fifth grade teacher should find books which are at the second, third, fourth, fifth, sixth, seventh, and eighth grade levels. Select a unit of material near the center of the book. Starting with the first word of each chapter, take each eighth word thereafter and place it in a column until 50 words have been written. These words should be double-spaced in large type and placed on a strip of heavy paper. Ask individual pupils to pronounce the words aloud.

A critical score of 42 should be established for each of the lists. If the student scores **more** than 45 proceed to the next higher grade level list. If the score is less than 47, proceed to the next **lower** grade level list. Continue the administration of the test until the score of 42–45 is reached. The approximate instructional reading level of the student with regard to vocabulary is at the level where the critical score was obtained on the instrument.

The materials used by the student in a given class should be at the critical level obtained on the test. This information can be used to plan lessons which will be helpful in aiding the student improve his/her sight word vocabulary and help the gifted reader reach his/her potential reading level.

It is possible to place the words on a transparency and use on the overhead projector for use with large groups.

The Informal Reading Analysis

The Informal Reading Analysis is a very useful strategy for use with individual students in assessing oral reading, word attack, and vocabulary. Comprehension proficiencies at the literal, interpretive, and critical levels can also be measured. The results of the inventory can be used in finding the most appropriate textbook for the gifted reader.

The analysis involves the use of selections from a graded series of books. One should find materials which are written about three grade levels above and three grade levels below the grade level of the student being tested. If the teacher utilizes the material with a seventh grade student, selections should be employed from books written at the fourth, fifth, sixth, seventh, eighth, ninth and tenth grade levels.

For the **oral reading portion** of the analysis, select a 100-word passage from the first third of each book and ask the student to pronounce each word. For complete accuracy, tape the oral reading and then listen carefully and record all types of errors. Each mistake counts one percentage point wrong. If the learner reads the material with 95 to 97 percent accuracy, the grade level of the material may be instructionally correct. If a score of less than 95 percent is obtained, the next lower level of material should be used until a score of 95–97 percent is reached. If a score of more than 95 percent is obtained on the first test, the next higher level should be utilized until the 95–97 percent score is obtained.

For the **silent reading comprehension section** of the analysis, select a 300-word passage from each of the materials for the student to read silently. The selection should come from the second half of the book being employed. Compile five questions for each selection. Questions should deal with such items as details, main ideas, critical reading, and drawing conclusions. A weight of 20 percentage points should be given to each question. For the material to be at the instructional reading level, the student must answer four of the five questions correctly. If all items are answered properly, the questions from the next **higher** level book should be used. If three or fewer questions are answered, the next **lower** level book should be used.

The level where the student scores four questions correct on the silent reading comprehension test should be considered the student's reading instructional level regardless of oral reading accuracy data. The oral reading score may be lower than the silent reading comprehension measure. Because silent reading comprehension is the end product of reading, the comprehension score is more important than oral reading performance.

The results of the *Informal Reading Analysis* can be most useful in determining if a given textbook is suitable for use with the gifted reader. If, for example, the readability of the book is at the fifth grade level and a student scores at the seventh grade instructional reading level on the test, one can assume that the text is too easy for the able reader. The level of the text should correspond with the instructional reading level of the student.

Reading Interests and Attitudes Survey

Information concerning a pupil's attitudes with respect to reading can be partially obtained from administering this survey and analyzing the responses. The sample items below are satisfactory for most gifted readers. They may need to be altered for use with older or younger students. A total of 10 to 20 statements should be used for the exercise. The following are examples of questions which may be used.

1. Reading is _____
2. I like reading when _____
3. The books I read are _____
4. Most books are _____
5. My favorite book is _____
6. Reading is fun when _____

When administering the test, explain to students that the information written on the sheets is confidential. What they write will help the teacher to become better acquainted with them. The students should respond to all items, but if they choose not to answer certain items, they should have that choice.

The information derived from the survey can be combined with responses obtained from verbal comments of the gifted reader to form a basis for altering the reading instructional program for the learner.

The Cloze Procedure

One of the most useful of all classroom reading assessment instruments is the cloze procedure. The tool can help assess a gifted student's ability in vocabulary, word attack, comprehension, and general reading skills. The procedure is constructed from using textbook material which is used in daily lessons. The following are steps to use in constructing the procedure.

1. Select a 260–280 word passage in the middle part of the class text or other source book.
2. On a piece of 8½″ by 11″ paper, type the first sentence word-by-word as it appears on the original copy.
3. Beginning with the second sentence, leave every fifth or sixth word blank until 50 blanks have been formulated.
4. Invite students to write a logical word on each blank.
5. Evaluate each student's paper allowing credit for each word that is the same as the one in the original text. No other words should be allowed for credit.

The teacher should use the following scoring standards.

26–50 correct — independent reading level. (The student is capable of reading a more difficult text.)
18–25 correct — instructional reading level. (The student can read this material at a satisfactory level with some help from the teacher.)
17–0 correct — frustration reading level. (The student cannot read this material satisfactorily even with the teacher help.

The cloze procedure should be administered using material from at least three different parts of the book. The decision concerning a pupil's reading ability should be based on a pattern of scores derived from several administrations.

The cloze strategy can also be used as a teaching device. Teachers of gifted readers may choose to undertake one or more of these activities.

1. Provide the students with copies of the technique with the 50 blanks. Place the list of 50 words which came from the book in a scrambled list. Pupils should select words from the list.

2. Invite pupils to write a word of their choice on the blanks. Ask them to read aloud their selection and listen carefully to note the differences in meaning used by each gifted reader.

3. Provide copies of the exercise and supply a multiple choice list of three words for each blank. One of the words should be the word from the original text, another word should be reasonably logical, and the third word should be totally unsuitable.

UTILIZING THE RESULTS OF
READING EVALUATION INSTRUMENTS

During the school year teachers compile a large amount of test data that relate to such aspects as grade equivalents, percentiles, stanines, scaled scores, and similar kinds of information. The information provided by computer test scoring services needs careful study if the needs of gifted readers are to be met. Three important principles to remember are:

1. **Study the commercial test manual carefully to derive accurate information regarding administration and scoring.** The company representative and school counselor or psychologist may also supply needed information. A careful understanding of the meaning of terms is important to insure that correct interpretations of the test are given to able readers and their parents.

2. **The analysis of the meaning of a test score should be made in the context of a pupil's background of experience, physical and emotional deficiencies, and other factors.** In some cases, a learner's emotional and/or physical status may create an invalid score on a test. The scores from several instruments should be used for instructional decisions.

3. **An item analysis of achievement tests should be made to determine the exact skill areas where the student may be able to improve.** The results of the test can be used for formulating the exact lessons needed by gifted readers for reaching their potential reading levels.

4. **One should remember that no one score from any one test is completely valid and reliable for making long range decisions about an able learner's future reading program.** The classroom teacher's careful observation of the student's daily oral and silent reading performance should serve as an important core of data for constructing units of instructional plans.

5. **Teachers should keep in mind that the most important purpose for conducting a program of evaluation is to improve instruction.** Lesson plans should be altered to the degree that evaluative data may suggest.

SUMMARY

Evaluation is a valuable aspect of the teaching-learning process for gifted readers since derived data from the various strategies provide the impetus for the construction and revision of the instructional program. There are numerous principles which should be remembered when utilizing evaluation tools and strategies such as the global approach to analysis that requires the use of a broad spectrum of approaches such as commercial and teacher-made tests, observation, and conversation with various learners. Tests should be selected with a number of criteria in mind. The program of instruction for gifted readers mandates a balanced program of evaluation strategies to assure that reading skill development is profitable and interesting. Helping each gifted reader to reach his or her potential reading letter should be an important goal of every teacher.

REFERENCES

1. Lien, Arnold J. *Measurement and Evaluation of Learning.* Dubuque, Wm. C. Brown Company Publishers, 1976, pp. 15–17.
2. Gronlund, Norman E. *Measurement and Evaluation in Teaching.* New York, Macmillan Publishing Co., Inc., 1981, pp. 5–6.
3. Mehrens, William A. and Irvin J. Lehmann. *Measurement and Evaluation in Education and Psychology* (Third Edition). New York, Holt, Rinehart and Winston, 1984, p. 5.
4. Cunningham, George K. *Educational and Psychological Measurement.* New York, Macmillan Publishing Company, 1986, p. 11.
5. Hill, Walter R. *Secondary School Reading: Process, Program, Procedure.* Boston, Allyn and Bacon, Inc., 1979, p. 90.
6. Spache, George D. and Evelyn B. Spache. *Reading in The Elementary School.* Boston, Allyn and Bacon, Inc., 1986, p. 567.
7. Smith, Richard J. and Dale D. Johnson. *Teaching Children To Read.* Reading, Addison-Wesley Publishing Company, 1976, p. 54.
8. Rubin, Dorothy. *Diagnosis and Correction in Reading Instruction.* New York, Holt, Rinehart and Winston, 1982, pp. 8–9.
9. Jongsma, Eugene A., "For Classroom Use," *Reading Teacher* 36(March, 1983), p. 724.
10. Heilman, Arthur W., Timothy R. Blair, and William H. Rupley. *Principles and Practices of Teaching Reading* (Sixth Edition). Columbus, Charles E. Merrill Publishing Company, 1986, p. 434.
11. Rubin, Dorothy. *Diagnosis and Correction in Reading Instruction.* New York, Holt, Rinehart and Winston, 1982, p. 11.

12. Bond, Guy L., Miles A. Tinker, and Barbara B. Wasson. *Reading Difficulties, Their Diagnosis and Correction* (Fourth Edition). Englewood Cliffs, Prentice-Hall, Inc., 1979, p. 62.

13. Lapp, Diane and James Flood. *Teaching Students To Read.* New York, Macmillan Publishing Company, 1986, p. 294.

14. Cunningham, Patricia M., Sharon Arthur Moore, James W. Cunningham, and David W. Moore. *Reading in Elementary Classrooms, Strategies and Observations.* New York, Longman, 1983, p. 195.

15. Lapp and Flood, op. cit., p. 285.

16. Gronlund, op. cit., p. 305.

17. Zintz, Miles V. and Zelda R. Maggart. *Corrective Reading* (Fifth Edition). Dubuque, Wm. C. Brown Publishers, 1986, p. 118.

18. Woodburn, Mary Stuart, "TEST REVIEW, New Macmillan Reading Analysis," *The Reading Teacher,* 40(November, 1986), pp. 204–206.

PERIODICALS FOR GIFTED READERS

Numerous periodicals for gifted young people are listed below. It is
the intent of the author to present a sampling of available resources,
but it is not meant to imply the personal endorsement of the featured
material. This information should be helpful in providing enrichment
and references on a multitude of reading levels. Complete addresses for
the publishers can be found in Appendix D.

Title	Publisher	Description
Ahoy, The Children's Magazine	Two Fathoms Publishing	This Canadian children's magazine contains excellent short stories, poems, puzzles, crafts, games and a regular review column.
American Health: Fitness of Body and Mind	American Health Partners	Young people who are interested in the many facets of health and nutrition will thoroughly enjoy reading this periodical.
American Poetry Review	World Poetry, Inc.	This periodical is both challenging and entertaining.
American Scientist	Sigma Xi, the Scientific Research Society	High school students with a special interest in science will find this research oriented magazine very informative.
Animal Kingdom	New York Zoological Society, Bronx Zoo	Wonderful articles on animals and conservation will inform and entertain the young reader.
The Antioch Review	Antioch Review, Inc.	Politics, current affairs and art are all featured in this fine magazine for all those

		who have an active interest in American culture.
Art and Man	U.S. Scholastic, Inc.	Children gifted in art will find this fullcolor periodical strives to help them understand the relationships between art, literature and culture. It is written for grades 7–12.
Astronomy Magazine	Astromedia Corp.	The world of the stars will come alive in this beautiful and popular magazine.
Audubon	National Audubon Society	This is a very worthwhile and prestigious magazine that stresses the importance of conservation.
Bow and Arrow	Gallent/Charger Publications	Young people will find that this excellent magazine stresses the fun aspects of bow hunting.
Boy's Life	Boy Scouts of America, Inc.	The child that loves nature and is interested in outdoor skills, fitness, hiking and camping will find the fiction and nonfiction stories very exciting.
Camp Fire Leadership	Camp Fire, Inc.	High School girls who are interested in increasing their leadership potential will find this magazine very rewarding and informative.
Cat Fancy	Fancy Publications	Cat enthusiasts will discover this monthly magazine to be interesting and complete with a wide variety of selections.
Changing Times	Kiplinger Washington Editors, Inc.	Children who are vitally interested in the subject of economics will find this magazine very profitable.
Chart Your Course	GCT Publishing Co., Inc.	This fine magazine contains original work by gifted,

		creative and talented children.
Chickadee	Young Naturalist	Children under the age of 8 will thoroughly enjoy this magazine because it is designed to stimulate their interest in the environment around them. It is an excellent publication from Canada.
Child Life	Child Life	Child Life provides a wonderful introduction to nutrition, health and exercise for children ages 5 to 12.
Children's Digest	Gruner & Jahr	Intended for children between the ages of 8 and 10, this wonderful magazine contains articles and stories dealing with the importance of health, nutrition, exercise and safety.
Children's Playmate, Youth Publications	The Saturday Evening Post Co.	There are a variety of topics and creative stories, poems and playlets in this magazine. It is written for ages 3 to 8.
Classroom Computer Learning	Learning Periodicals Group	This magazine contains pull-out posters and two directories of educational computer programs.
Cobblestone	Cobblestone Publishing	In this exciting magazine, children will find stories of our American history. It is intended for ages 8 to 14.
College Board Review	College Entrance Examination Board	Going from high school to college is the main topic of this general education magazine.
Creative Computing, Computer Notes	Ziff Davis Publishing	The world of computers will unfold as readers gain insight into applications for personal computers.

Cricket, The Magazine for Children	Open Court Publishing	Children ages 6 to 12 will enjoy the high quality selection of literature as well as the excellent ideas for crafts.
Curious Naturalist	Massachusetts Audubon Society	The articles in this magazine are designed for the young naturalist.
Discovery	Light & Life Press	Many hours of leisuretime reading will await a young child. Fascinating articles, crafts, poetry and puzzles are incorporated into a very successful format.
Dynamite	Scholastic, Inc.	Children will find this fast-paced magazine to be exciting reading.
The Electric Company Magazine	Children's Television Workshop	The goal of this periodical is to help children improve their reading skills.
Enter	Children's Television Workshop	Computer skills and technology are the major topics of this excellent magazine. It is written especially for children 10 to 16.
Faces, The Magazine About People	Cobblestone Publishing, Inc.	Written in cooperation with the American Museum of Natural History, this publication is for children ages 8 to 14 who enjoy studying cultural anthropology.
Highlights	Highlights for Children	This respected magazine contains excellent stories and articles for very enjoyable reading.
Hot Dog	Scholastic, Inc.	The wide variety of articles in this magazine provides fascinating reading enjoyment.

Humpty Dumpty	Benjamin Franklin Literary & Medical Society	Children who are beginning readers will enjoy the fascinating stories, poems, games and puzzles.
Isaac Asimov's Science Fiction Magazine	Davis Readers Group	The creative short stories, articles, profiles and poems make this periodical very popular for all science fiction enthusiasts.
Jack and Jill	Benjamin Franklin Literary & Medical Society	Health, nutrition and safety are just a few of the topics covered in this respected magazine for children.
Jam Magazine	Jam Magazine/Ltd.	Jam is a Canadian magazine designed to delight children ages 10–15. The issues contain a variety of interesting topics.
K–Power	Scholastic, Inc.	Pre-teen and teen computer users will find the emphasis on applications very helpful.
National Geographic	National Geographic Society	This distinguished and colorful magazine will interest the entire family.
National Geographic World	National Geographic Society	Children who are interested in nature will love this colorful and informative magazine.
Nautica, The Magazine of the Sea for Young People	Spinnaker Press, Inc.	This periodical provides articles on sea creatures, sea-lore, sea science, sea history and sea sports.
Odyssey	Astromedia Corp.	Young people will enjoy the variety of information on astronomy and space science offered in this publication.
Owl	Scholastic, Inc.	The main objective of this magazine is to stimulate children to learn more about their environment.

Penny Power	Consumers Union of U.S. Inc.	Teaching children about consumer education is the goal of this publication. It provides product rating and consumer advice for young people (ages 8 to 14) from Consumer Reports.
Puns Upon a Time	Fandon Unlimited Enterprises	Humorous science fiction and fantasy stories make this magazine delightful reading.
Ranger Rick	National Wildlife Federation, Inc.	The photography and articles provide a wonderful method to teach children about nature and conservation.
R/C Modeler	R/C Modeler Corp.	If airplanes and flying fascinate a reader, he/she will thoroughly enjoy this publication. Special emphasis is placed on aircraft construction and includes informative, how-to articles for building different radar controlled model airplanes.
Scholastic News Citizen	Scholastic, Inc.	Children find this excellent publication helps them to explore their world.
Science Digest	Hearst Corp.	This publication provides the latest news in science, technology and medicine complete with explanatory articles, picture stories, columns and features.
Scienceland	Scienceland	Geared for the very young child, this picture book nurtures scientific thinking.
Science World	Scholastic, Inc.	Young people in grades 7 to 10 will enjoy the many articles on general science, nature study, earth and space science and technological advances.

Sea Child	Spinnaker Press, Inc.	The wonders of the sea are introduced to children ages 5 to 8.
Smithsonian	Smithsonian Institution	People enjoy this distinguished magazine because it is a broadly based special interest periodical. The main topics are history, American culture, natural and the hard sciences.
Softside	Softside/Software	Young people who enjoy working with computers will find this magazine extremely useful.
Turtle Magazine for Preschool Kids	Benjamin Franklin Literary & Medical Society, Inc.	Preschool children will enjoy learning about health, safety, nutrition and exercise.
Wee Wisdom	Unity School of Christianity	This publication is designed to inspire children to have a good self-image and gain an appreciation for all aspects of life.
WOW	Scholastic, Inc.	Geared for children ages 4–9, this periodical helps provide play as well as activity ideas.

ANNOTATED PROFESSIONAL BOOK LIST
FOR TEACHERS OF GIFTED CHILDREN

1. Alexander, Patricia A. and Joseph A. Muia. *Gifted Education: A Comprehensive Roadmap.* Rockville, Aspen Systems Corporation, 1982.

   Beginning with a historical account of the gifted movement, the authors express their concern about gifted education in the United States. Important topics such as acquiring funds and understanding current legislature are discussed. A special section on learning style and content is very valuable.

2. Baker, D. Philips and David R. Bender. *Library Media Programs and the Special Learner.* Hamden, Connecticut, Library Professional Publications, 1981.

   An excellent chapter is included in this text on gifted and talented exemplary programs. The authors discuss the major factors that must be included. Guidelines are given for establishing gifted programs as well as criteria for selecting individuals that should participate.

3. Baskin, Barbara H. and Karen H. Harris. *Books for the Gifted Child.* New York, R.R. Bowker Company, 1980.

   The authors chart the intellectual aspects of the reading experience and provide a selected guide to intellectually demanding books. The list includes a wide variety of topics.

4. Clark, Barbara. *Growing Up Gifted* (2nd Edition). Columbus, Charles E. Merrill Publishing Company, 1983.

   This volume provides a general overview of gifted education with special emphasis on a model to integrate the cognitive, social-emotional, physical, and intuitive growth of the learner. Teachers will find the book to be an excellent addition to their resource libraries.

5. Clark, Barbara. *Optimizing Learning The Integrative Education Model In The Classroom.* Columbus, Charles E. Merrill Publishing Company, 1986.

   Dr. Clark outlines a model for educational reform by discussing such topics as the total brain and mind for learning; creating a learning environment; sharing the responsibility for learning; and using cognitive processes. The strategies and lessons described in Chapter 9 provide the teacher with practical suggestions for building integrative lessons for preschoolers, elementary pupils, and high school students.

6. Clark, Gilbert and Enid Zimmerman. *Educating Artistically Talented Students.* Syracuse, Syracuse University Press, 1984.

   This unique and most unusual volume addresses a number of issues which should be considered seriously by all educators who prescribe instructional programs for those students who are identified as artistically talented. The important aspects of identification, teaching strategies, curriculum content, and administrative arrangements are discussed thoroughly from the standpoints of research results and pragmatic observations. The last section dealing with suggestions and recommendations for present and future curriculum decisions with regard to these pupils is especially useful.

7. Clendening, Corinne P. and Ruth Ann Davies. *Challenging The Gifted: Curriculum Enrichment and Acceleration Models.* New York, R.R. Bowker Company, 1983.

   This text is a valuable asset for improving any reading program related to the gifted. The examples for a successful reading enrichment and acceleration program will help any teacher. The authors explore topics to provide a sound background for the gifted child. A list is given of fascinating bibliographies of many gifted authors.

8. Cox, June, Neil Daniel, and Bruce O. Boston. *Educating Able Learners Programs and Promising Practices.* Austin, University of Texas Press, 1985.

   The authors undertook and completed the Richardson Foundation Study and describe the results of the effort through a discussion of the important aspects of gifted education including current curriculum approaches, what works best, and strategies to help insure a comprehensive program of instruction which provides for flexible pacing, acceleration, and enrichment. The most valuable section of the volume for many readers is the summary of recommendations made relating to administering programs, discovering talent, and developing staff competencies and overall support for the program.

9. Davis, Gary A. and Sylvia B. Rimm. *Education of The Gifted and Talented.* Englewood Cliffs, Prentice-Hall, 1985.

   Some of the major topics included in this important volume are program planning, grouping and counseling, curriculum models, the handicapped gifted child, and program evaluation. One of the most valuable segments of the book is Chapter 16 which deals with many suggestions offered to parents of gifted children for helping young learners develop to the maximum level of their potential. The bill of rights for parents of gifted children is especially meaningful.

10. Ehrlich, Virginia Z. *Gifted Children: A Guide For Parents and Teachers.* Englewood Cliffs, Prentice-Hall, 1982.

    People wishing to update their knowledge in the field of gifted education will want to read this volume. It is written for both parents and teachers and skillfully defines the role of parents and teachers in gifted education. An excellent section lists career opportunities for the gifted and talented. The final part of the book discusses the legal ramifications of the Gifted and Talented Children's Education Act of 1978.

11. Feldhusen, John (Editor). *Toward Excellence in Gifted Education.* Denver, Love Publishing Company, 1985.

Six outstanding authorities in the field of gifted education discuss several significant areas of instruction including the conception of the field of gifted education; philosophies and approaches; appropriate curriculum; identification and assessment; key administrative concepts; facilitators for gifted learners; helping a child toward individual excellence; and evaluating gifted programs. The volume presents a short, yet comprehensive, view of gifted education.

12. Fox, Lynn H., Linda Brody, and Dianne Tobin. *Learning-Disabled/Gifted Children: Identification and Programming.* Baltimore, University Park Press, 1983.

Combined in this book is a collection of articles that deal with both learning-disabled and gifted education. Topics such as the gifted child with a learning disability and models for identifying giftedness make this text an excellent resource book for readers wishing to gain insight into these subjects. Chapter 11 provides pertinent information about the use of computers in gifted programs.

13. Gallagher, James J., et al. *Leadership Unit: The Use of Teacher-Scholar Teams to Develop Units for the Gifted.* New York, Trillium Press, 1982.

This is a challenging book designed to aid teacher-scholar teams in developing units for the gifted. Of major concern is the importance of providing valid, systematic programs that recognize the following characteristics of the gifted: advanced ability to relate one idea to another, advanced ability to make sound judgments, and the ability to comprehend larger systems of knowledge. A special curriculum unit on leadership is included for the gifted and talented student at the upper elementary and junior high level.

14. Gallagher, James J. *Teaching The Gifted Child* (3rd Edition). Boston, Allyn and Bacon, 1985.

The author has added many new subject areas to his nationally-known book which was first published in 1964. Educators will find the sections relating to suggestions for instructing gifted pupils in the various content areas to be especially valuable. A discussion of the status of current state and federal programs for the gifted is included along with important suggestions for the professional preparation of educators for the gifted.

15. Grossi, John A. *Model State Policy, Legislation and State Plan Toward the Education of Gifted and Talented Students: A Handbook for State and Local Districts.* Reston, The Council for Exceptional Children, 1980.

This is a very comprehensive text for any group planning to establish a gifted program. It contains valuable information that is needed when organizing a program. Guidance is given in writing formal definitions of the term "gifted" as well as help in fairly assessing a student population.

16. Heimberger, Mary. *Teaching the Gifted and Talented in the Elementary Classroom.* Washington, D.C., National Education Association of the United States, 1980.

The author has published an important book for any teacher who wishes to challenge gifted students. Half of the book is devoted to reading and the gifted. Creative ideas are included for vocabulary development, listening, oral expression, literary appreciation, and written composition. It is very helpful in providing insight to this challenge.

17. Howley, Aimee, Craig B. Howley, and Edwina D. Pendarvis. *Teaching Gifted Children Principles and Strategies.* Boston, Little, Brown, and Company, 1986.

The major emphases of this important volume focus on assessment and interpretation, instructional procedures, and social implications. Valuable information is provided for the reader regarding enrichment techniques and modification of behavior strategies which will result in a maximum level of learning for the gifted pupil. Unique for volumes of this nature is a pointed discussion of the political economy of gifted education in this country.

18. Humphrey, James H. *Teaching Gifted Children Through Motor Learning.* Springfield, Charles C Thomas, Publisher, 1985.

For 25 years the author has studied the phenomenon of how children learn through motor activity. In the book he covers the cognitive theory of motor learning and explores how gifted children can learn about reading, science, and mathematics through motor activity. Also included is a section on identification of the gifted child.

19. Jackson, David M. *Curriculum Development for the Gifted.* Guilford, Special Learning Corporation, 1980.

Jackson's book is excellent for anyone considering constructing a gifted program in their school. Challenging articles are included that are designed to give insight into the complexities of the curriculum design needed for success. Examples are given of the screening-identification process as well as locations of support for the teacher. A special section contains frequently asked questions of parents of gifted students.

20. Karnes, Frances A. and Emily C. Collins. *Assessment in Gifted Education.* Springfield, Charles C Thomas, Publisher, 1981.

This is a valuable resource book for teachers looking for assessment criteria that will aid in the identification of gifted students in their schools. The information on each testing measure includes the test's name, author, distributor, date of publication, grade or ages of students, validity measurement, reliability, and areas actually assessed during the test.

21. Karnes, Frances A. and Emily C. Collins. *Handbook of Instructional*

Resources and References for Teaching the Gifted. Boston, Allyn and Bacon, Inc., 1982.

The authors have produced a wonderful resource book for all teachers who are in the process of selecting and adapting challenging materials for their gifted programs. Special emphasis has been placed on material that will enhance the learning experience.

22. Karnes, Merle B. (Editor). *The Underserved: Our Young Gifted Children.* Reston, The Council for Exceptional Children, 1983.

Several national authorities such as Allan Shwedel, Kippy Abroms, Andrew Gunsberg, Mark Williams, and the editor, Merle B. Karnes, contributed valuable articles to this well-known publication. Some of the topics discussed include identification procedures, conceptual models, types of teachers needed, affective development, the role of the family, and evaluation strategies. The editor discusses the challenges facing educators for providing an educational program for gifted children which is based on their precise needs and abilities.

23. Kitano, Margie K. and Darrell F. Kirby. *Gifted Education, A Comprehensive View.* Boston, Little, Brown and Company, 1986.

The authors present a thorough overview of a total program for educating gifted learners with special emphasis given to a broad perspective of theory, research, methods, and curriculum which are appropriate for these children. Practical strategies are presented relating to placement procedures and methods for enhancing inductive, creative, and evaluative thinking.

24. Labuda, Michael. *Creative Reading for Gifted Learners: A Design for Excellence.* Newark, International Reading Association, 1980.

The many contributing authors in this collection of short essays all have the common goal of improving gifted educational opportunities for children. Important issues such as the parents' role in fostering reading as well as using creative reading in the intermediate and secondary grade levels are explored. The prospects of gifted reading educational programs for the future are examined.

25. Leyden, Susan. *Helping The Child of Exceptional Ability.* London, Croom Heim, 1985.

This outstanding British volume deals with numerous aspects of gifted education which are applicable for both British and American educators. The author describes in detail the important characteristics of young gifted children as they move from the infant and pre-school years to the intermediate and advanced levels. Special attention is given to those strategies and practices which are necessary if a climate of educational growth is to be established for these kinds of children.

26. Maier, Norah. *Teaching the Gifted, Challenging the Average.* Toronto, Governing Council of the University of Toronto, 1982.

Collections of unique articles are covered in this text. It contains valuable information for dealing with the gifted child. An entire chapter is devoted to the importance of reading as well as practical suggestions for challenging creative topics with regard to the entire class. The authors firmly believe that situations that can benefit the gifted child can also enhance the learning of the rest of the class.

27. Meyen, Edward L. *Basic Reading in the Study of Exceptional Children and Youth.* Denver, Love Publishing Company, 1980.

    The fifth chapter of this book deals exclusively with the gifted student. Excellent articles such as program planning for the gifted, developing values in gifted children, and teacher preparation for the gifted make this book a valuable resource for anyone planning curriculum improvements.

28. Mitchell, Patricia Bryce (Editor). *A Policymaker's Guide to Issues In Gifted and Talented Education.* Washington, D.C., National Association of State Boards of Education, 1981.

    Addressed to those who are concerned with gifted education, this booklet has excellent sections dealing exclusively with policy making as well as suggestions for making these decisions. A number of state profiles are given as examples of well written programs that have been successful.

29. Mitzel, Carol. *Encyclopedia of Educational Research.* New York, The Macmillan Company, 1982.

    An excellent section is included in this fine text about recent research on gifted children as well as creativity. The volume would be a valuable addition to the professional library of any school.

30. Morgan, Harry J. and Carolyn G. Tennant and Milton J. Gold. *Elementary and Secondary Level Programs for the Gifted and Talented.* New York, Columbia University, 1980.

    This work is excellent to use when organizing a gifted program. Two types of approaches are discussed, intra classroom and extra classroom. When developing the curriculum, the Tannenbaum and the Renzulli approaches are explained. Valuable ideas are given for designing special schools and summer programs. Possible options concerning acceleration through school and early admission into college are of interest.

31. Painter, Frieda. *Living With A Gifted Child.* London, Souvenir Press, 1984.

    While this book is intended primarily for British parents of gifted children, it is also a source of very practical information for educators from any country. Numerous strategic topics are included such as identification procedures, selection of the proper school, parents' rights, and career prospects. The checklists and informal inventories are particularly useful for all persons involved in educational programs for the gifted.

32. Perrone, Philip A. and Robert A. Male. *The Developmental Education and Guidance of Talented Learners.* Rockville, Aspen Systems Corporation, 1981.

    Meeting the unique developmental needs of talented children and adolescents is the major thrust of this text. The book has sections with guidelines for identifying gifted students as well as establishing appropriate programs. Also included are general strategies for teaching the talented and those with talent potential.

33. Polette, Nancy. *Picture Books for Gifted Programs.* Metuchen, N.J., The Scarecrow Press, 1981.

    This book provides excellent references for any teacher in search of available materials for gifted programs. There are valuable sections dealing with communication skills as well as methods that challenge productive and critical thinking in students.

34. Polette, Nancy. *3R's For The Gifted.* Littleton, Libraries Unlimited, 1982.

    The author includes an overall explanation of the characteristics of the gifted child and the curriculum which should be established for these pupils. Special sections are provided for the detailed descriptions of reading, writing, and research modules which should be utilized with all pupils from the kindergarten to the intermediate levels. All of the activities are easy to use and challenge each learner to work at his/her maximum level of learning.

35. Swassing, Raymond H. *Teaching Gifted Children and Adolescents.* Columbus, Charles E. Merrill Publishing Company, 1985.

    Several important topics are included in this work which should prove to be informative and stimulating to all educators who work with gifted learners. Precise strategies are described for teaching mathematics, science, social studies, reading, and writing to gifted pupils of all ages. Part Three of the book is especially interesting since it provides valuable information relating to such matters as using computers, career preparation, methods of developing creativity, and program implementation and evaluation.

36. Tannenbaum, Abraham J. *Gifted Children Psychological and Educational Perspectives.* New York, Macmillan Publishing Company, Inc., 1983.

    Tannenbaum's volume is designed to be a textbook for undergraduate and graduate courses in gifted education. All of the basic aspects of giftedness are included in the volume such as the history of the gifted, defining giftedness, theories of creativity, nurturing high potential, building enrichment programs, and evaluating programs for the gifted. The survey of feelings about the gifted and their education should prove highly useful to all school personnel.

37. Treffinger, Donald, Robert L. Hohn and John F. Feldhusen. *Reach Each You Teach.* Buffalo, DOK Publishers, 1981.

    The authors have designed a versatile handbook for teachers of the gifted. Individual learning is a major objective with a special section geared to improve planning and organization skills. A final section stresses the evaluation process.

38. Tuttle, Frederick and Lawrence A. Becker. *Program Design and Develop-*

ment for Gifted and Talented Students. Washington, D.C., National Education Association of the United States, 1980.

This is a very informative text that covers almost all the major concerns in forming a gifted program. Topics such as program design, curricular models, teacher selection, and program evaluation are all discussed in depth. A section is included that goes through the "how-to" steps of initiating a gifted program in any area. The book contains excellent examples of administrative designs and curricular models.

39. Tuttle, Frederick B., Jr., and Laurence A. Becker. *Characteristics and Identification of Gifted and Talented Students* (2nd Edition). Washington, D.C., National Education Association, 1983.

The goal of this volume is to give step-by-step instructions regarding the building of a gifted program. Pertinent information regarding the formation of a workable definition of gifted programs are included. Sample checklists, questionnaires, and inventories also make this a valuable resource book.

40. Van Tassel-Baska, Joyce. *An Administrator's Guide to The Education of Gifted and Talented Children.* Washington, D.C., National Association of State Boards of Education, 1981.

This booklet is designed to guide administrators who wish to establish programs for the gifted and talented. A brief historical account of gifted education in America as well as testing techniques used to identify students are outlined. An excellent section is included that aids in evaluating potential programs.

41. West, Nancy (Editor). *Annual Editions—Educating Exceptional Children 82/83.* Guilford, Dushkin Publishing Group, Inc., 1983.

In Section 9 of this edition are five excellent articles dealing with the current concerns of anyone working with the gifted. Of special importance is a comprehensive look at gifted education in the future including a valuable section on the importance of reading.

42. Whitmore, Joanne Rand. *Giftedness, Conflict and Underachievement.* Boston, Allyn and Bacon, Inc., 1980.

This text provides an overview of recent research. The author concentrates on the problems of highly gifted underachievers. All teachers would benefit from reading about the new trends in gifted education.

INSTRUCTIONAL MATERIALS
FOR GIFTED STUDENTS

This list is a sample of available materials which may assist a teacher of gifted students. The listing of an item does not necessarily imply a personal endorsement of the author for a given selection. The use of a material on a pilot basis may be a practical procedure to employ. Complete addresses for the publishers can be found in Appendix D.

AUDIO-VISUAL MATERIAL

Publisher	Title	Grade Level	Description
Educational Reading Services	First Start Read-Along Program	1–4	Large type with simple, exciting stories makes this a wonderful book/cassette series.
Educational Reading Services	Learn-About Book Bags	2–4	The book bag series help teach children about the wonders of nature. Also included is a word-for-word cassette that enhances their reading experience.
Educational Reading Services	Talking Picture Dictionary	1–4	Learning is made fun through the use of the Talking Dictionary. Children learn the sounds of letters and words as well as discovering the relationships between words.
Instructional Communications Technology, Inc.	Critical Reading Program	2–6	Improved reading comprehension is the major objective of this fine series. The entire series contains

38 cassette sets that permit
read-along practice.

COMPUTER PROGRAMS

Publisher	Title	Grade Level	Description
American Guidance Service	MicroSoc Thinking Games		The computer programs are content rich, yet easy-to-operate games. The software helps your child understand language concepts and develop vital problemsolving abilities.
Barnell Loft, Ltd.	Reading Through the Fourth Dimension	4–12	These computer programs are very useful for providing enrichment or independent practice. The two diskettes include some of the following: pronouns-personal, interrogative, indefinite, signal words, and cause and effect sequences.
Barnell Loft, Ltd.	Word Theater	4–9	In this fine software package there are a total of eight diskettes. Each diskette has a total of 150 skits that are designed to improve comprehension vocabulary and writing skills.
Follett Library Book Co.	Alphakey	K–3	Young students will enjoy learning the alphabet on the computer's keyboard. After typing the correct letter, the child is rewarded with a smiling face. There is no attempt to teach finger position.
Follett Library Book Co.	Juggles' Rainbow	Pre-school to 1	Disguised as fun in in this computer program are pre-reading skills and computer basics. They will be learning

			the concepts of above/below and left/right as they generate patterns with the graphics.
Follett Library Book Co.	Letter Recognition	K–1	This program not only introduces the child to the computer but also helps develop letter recognition. The program options include upper case letters only, lower case letters only, numerals, or mixed characters.
Follett Library Books Co.	Opposites	1–10	Designed to increase your child's vocabulary this computer program can use the words provided or you can add your own words.
Follett Library Books Co.	Rapid Reader	7–12	Increased reading speed and comprehension are the main objectives of this fine computer program. The program can display up to 2,000 words per minute. The word banks can be modified to suit your taste.
Follett Library Books Co.	Reading for Meaning with Mother Goose	2–4	The two program disks includes over 60 separate rhymes. The question section requires the child to identify details, sequence of events, predict outcomes and identify main ideas.
Follett Library Books Co.	Return-To-Reading Library	4–12	Based on the most widely read books in the curriculum, this computer program is designed to be used *after* students have read the correlated books.
Follett Library Books Co.	Wizard of Words	1–12	Using a powerful dictionary of over 38,000 words, this computer program has five different word games to im-

			prove your child's language learning skills.
The Continental Press, Inc.	Cause and Effect	3–5	A fascinating computer program that develops cause and effect relationships.
The Continental Press, Inc.	Extra! Extra!	Ages 8 and up	The computer helps students to uncover the "facts" for a newspaper story. This unique program offers three skill levels and over 60 different news stories. The objective is to encourage quick, accurate fact finding.
The Continental Press, Inc.	Fact or Opinion	2–3.5	A game board format provides a unique format that helps students make distinctions between facts and opinions.
The Continental Press, Inc.	Speed Reader II	7 and up	Six lessons are provided in this computer program that will train students in established techniques for increasing reading speed and proficiency.

SPECIAL INTEREST TOPICS

Publisher	Title	Grade Level	Description
Barnell Loft, Ltd.	Profiles of Black Americans	Books 1, 2 & 3	Each book consists of 96 pages and is filled with the many accomplishments of black Americans. The profiles consist of prominent educators, athletes, scientists, entertainers and authors.
Crestwood House, Inc.	Funseekers Series	3–4	The wonderful world of reading adventure awaits your child in these fine action-packed stories.

Crestwood House, Inc.	Wildlife (Habits and Habitat)	5–6	Children that are fascinated by nature will love reading about these well-known, but little understood animals. These are written from a conservationist's viewpoint.
Educators Publishing Service	Return to Aztlan	4–8	Mexican history from 8,000 BC to the Revolution of 1910 is discussed in this fine book.
Educators Publishing Service	The Story of Western Civilization	4–8	The Story of Western Civilization is a series of three illustrated reading workbooks. The three titles are "How Civilization Began," "Greece and Rome Build Great Civilization" and "The Middle Ages."
Fearon Teacher Aids	Creative Activities For The Gifted Child	1–6	Over 100 ideas are listed to help you motivate your gifted students.
Fearon Teacher Aids	Do Something Different	5–8	This unique manual provides step-by-step instructions to such activities as publishing a magazine, running a snack bar business, and curating a classroom museum.
Fearon Teacher Aids	Inventors Workshop	3–8	Mystery, illusion and humor team up with basic science principles to help kids take gadgets apart, build oddball contraptions and much much more.
Fearon Teacher Aids	Mind Stretchers	1–6	Two levels of challenge are provided to help the gifted stretch their imaginations with captivating codes, paper puzzles, story starters and unique memory games.
Fearon Teacher Aids	100 Activities for Gifted	1–6	Practical ideas are provided to motivate the gifted

| | Children | | student to apply their talents in work-related areas. |
| Fearon Teacher Aids | The Creativity Catalog | 4–8 | The gifted child will love the 30 projects for creating cartoons, picture books, and T.V. shows as well as the practical information about careers in acting, writing and much more. |

MISCELLANEOUS

Publisher	Title	Grade Level	Description
Barnell Loft, Ltd.	The Incredible Series	Ages 9–16	A wonderful action packed series of stories that will gain and maintain the interest of the gifted reader. The entire series consists of 13 books.
Educational Reading Services	Children's Classics	4–6	This is a collection of well-loved classics that is beautifully illustrated to invite children to read and cultivate an early taste for good literature.
Educational Reading Services	Easy-To-Read Mysteries	2–4	Children with inquiring minds will enjoy this series of easy-to-read mysteries spiced with the touch of humor children enjoy most.
Educational Reading Services	On The Wings of Pegasus	3–6	This collection consists of a treasury of myths, legends, folklore, and humor that helps give children a taste of fine literature.
Educational Reading Services	Paths to Adventure	5–8	This fine collection of adventure books promotes reading as a source of wonderful entertainment.
Educational Reading Services	Read, Read, Read	6–9	Leisure reading for the gifted child can be greatly

			enhanced by this fine collection of short books.
Fearon Teacher Aids	Alphabet Stories		Your young child will find he alphabet characters come to life through the magic of picture stories.
Macmillan Publishing Co., Inc.	Macmillan Literary Heritage	7–12	In this collection of short stories by famous authors of the past and present the student will find exercises to increase vocabulary as well as questions designed for discussion and composition.
Troll Associates	Troll Read-Along	2–5	A wonderful variety of stories are included in this fascinating series. Each set contains 10 books of one topic.

TEACHING AIDS

Publisher	Title	Grade Level	Description
American Guidance Service	High Hat Early Reading Programs	Pre-school to Grade 1	This series makes possible a wealth of coordinated visual and verbal activities. Children learn to acticulate single sounds correctly and blend sounds into syllables and words.
Barnell Loft, Ltd.	Developing Key Concepts in Comprehension	1–10	This exciting series stresses four key classes of ideas: identical, related, unrelated, and contradictory ideas. The series not only enhances their reading ability but also their ability to write with clarity.
Educators Publishing Service	Aptitude Tests in Reading Comprehension for College Entrance	11–12	Students nearing the completion of high school will benefit from this fine manual. Practice is provided to improve reading speed

			and comprehension. Tips are also provided to improve performance on exams.
Educators Publishing Service	Independent Reading Exercises to Improve Reading Speed, Comprehension, Vocabulary, Retention and Critical Thinking		Practical techniques are provided to aid the student in developing better comprehension.
Educators Publishing Service	Reading for Content and Speed	3–6	Children will find that the series of four books will improve their reading comprehension and speed.
Educators Publishing Service	Reasoning and Reading Level 1, Level 2	Level 1 6–9 Level 2 8–9	The main focus of the the workbook is to illustrate the kinds of thinking students need to do when they want to understand and evaluate what they read.
Fearon Teacher Aids	Reading Power Plus		Vocabulary, decoding, and comprehension are the three main objectives in this fine workbook.
Jamestown Publishers	Learning To Study	3–8	A very valuable skill for any child is to learn to be able to study effectively. This helpful series provides study strategies that will aid your child.
Jamestown Publishers	Skimming & Scanning	Middle Level, Advanced Level	The goal of this text is to improve the reading skills of the learner.
Instructional Fair, Inc.	Reading Comprehension	2–8	There are 40 original high-interest stories involving science, nature, legends and myths. The stories are accompanied by teacher-

			created activities that test comprehension and stimulate thinking.
Instructional Fair, Inc.	Readiness Skills	Ages 4–6	This "Little Book" series was designed to develop the readiness skills of pre-school to kindergarten age children. Language skills, concept development and following directions are stressed throughout the book.

APPENDIX D

LIST OF PUBLISHERS AND THEIR ADDRESSES

Addison-Wesley Publishing Company, Inc. Jacob Way, Reading, Massachusetts 01867

Aims Instructional Media, Inc., 626 Justin Avenue, Glendale, California 91201

Alfred Higgins Productions, 9100 Sunset Boulevard, Los Angeles, California 90069

Alfred A. Knopf, Inc. 201 East 50th Street, New York, New York, 10022

Allyn and Bacon, 470 Atlantic Avenue, Boston, Massachusetts 02210

American Educational Computer, Inc. 2450 Embarcadero Way, Palo Alto, California 94303

American Guidance Service, Publisher's Building, P.O. Box 99, Circle Pines, Minnesota 55014-1796

American Health Partners, 80 Fifth Avenue, New York, New York 10011

Antioch Review, Inc., P.O. Box 148, Yellow Springs, Ohio 45387

Aspen Systems Corporation, 1600 Research Boulevard, Rockville, Maryland 20850

Astromedia Corp., 625 East St. Paul Avenue, Box 92788, Milwaukee, Wisconsin 53202

Audio-Visual Research Company, P.O. Box 71, Waseca, Minnesota 56093

A.V. Concepts Corporation, 30 Montauk Boulevard, Oakdale, New York 11769

Barnell Loft, Ltd., 958 Church Street, Baldwin, New York 11510

Benjamin Franklin Literary & Medical Society, Inc., 1100 Waterway Boulevard, Box 567, Indianapolis, Indiana 46206

Boy Scouts of America, Inc., 1325 Walnut Hill Lane, Irving, Texas 75602

Borg-Warner Educational System, 600 West University Drive, Arlington Heights, Illinois 60004

BFA Educational Media, P.O. Box 1795, 2211 Michigan Avenue, Santa Monica, California 90406

Brain Bank, Inc., P.O. Box 1708, Greenville, Texas 75401

Brigham Young University, Media Marketing, Provo, Utah 84602

William C. Brown Company, 2460 Kerper Boulevard, Dubuque, Iowa 52001

California Test Bureau, McGraw-Hill, Del Monte Research Park, Monterey, California 93940

Camp Fire, Inc., 4601 Madison Avenue, Kansas City, Missouri 64112

Cardinal Software, 13646 Jefferson Davis Highway, Woodbridge, Virginia 22191

Charles Merrill Publishing Company, 1300 Alum Creek Drive, Columbus, Ohio 43216

Charles C Thomas, Publisher, 2600 South First Street, Springfield, Illinois 62794

Child Life, 1100 Waterway Boulevard, 567B, Indianapolis, Indiana 46202

Children's Television Workshop, One Lincoln Plaza, New York, New York 10023

Cobblestone Publishing, Inc., 20 Grove Street, Peterborough, New Hampshire 03458

College Entrance Examination Board, 888 Seventh Avenue, New York, New York 10106

Committee on Diagnostic Reading Tests, Mountain Home, North Carolina 28758

Computer Assisted Instruction, Inc. 6115 28th Street, S.E., Grand Rapids, Michigan 45506

Computer Courseware Company, 2118 South Grand Avenue, Santa Ana, California 92705

Computer Curriculum Corporation, 1070 Arastradero Road, P.O. Box 10080, Palo Alto, California 94303

Computer Island, 227 Hampton Green, Staten Island, New York 10312

Consumers Union of U.S. Inc., 256 Washington Street, Mt. Vernon, New York 10553

The Continental Press, Inc., Elizabethtown, Pennsylvania 17022

Coronet Films and Video, 108 Wilmot Road, Deerfield, Illinois 60015

Creative Curriculum, Inc./Computer Courseware, Inc.

Crestwood House, Highway 66 South, Box 3427, Mankato, Minnesota 56002-3427

Croft, Inc. 4601 York Road, Baltimore, Maryland 21212

Curriculum Associates, Inc. 5 Esquire Road, North Billerica, Massachusetts 01821

Data Command of Imperial International Learning Corp., P.O. Box 272, Fairfield, Ohio 45014

Davis Readers Group, 380 Lexington Avenue, New York, New York 10017

Developmental Learning Materials, 7440 Natchez Avenue, Niles, Illinois 60648

Walt Disney Educational Media Company, 500 South Buena Vista Street, Burbank, California 91521

DLM Teaching Resources, P.O. Box 4000, One DLM Park, Allen, Texas 75002

DOK Publishers, 71 Radcliffe Road, Buffalo, New York 14214

Dushkin Publishing Group, Inc., Sluice Dock, Guilford, Connecticut 06437

Economy Company Individualized Instruction Incorporated, P.O. Box 25308, 1901 North Walnut, Oklahoma City, Oklahoma 73125

Edmark Corporation, P.O. Box 3903, Bellevue, Washington 98009

Education Activities, Inc., Box 392, Freeport, New York 11520

Educational Developmental Laboratories, Inc., 1221 Avenue of the Americas, New York, New York 10020

Educational Reading Services, 320 State Highway 17, Mahwah, New Jersey 07430

Educators Publishing Service, Inc., 75 Moulton Street, Cambridge, Massachusetts 02238

Educulture, Inc., One Dubuque Plaza, Suite 730, Dubuque, Iowa 52001

EMC Publishing Changing Times Education Service, 180 East Sixth Street, Saint Paul, Minnesota 60607

ESP, Inc., Box 5037, Jonesboro, Arkansas 72403

Fancy Publications, Inc., Box 4030, San Clemente, California 92672

Fandom Unlimited Enterprises, Box 70868, Sunnyvale, California 94069

Fearon Teacher Aids, 19 Davis Drive, Belmont, California 94002

Follett Library Book Co., 4506 Northwest Highway, Crystal Lake, Illinois 60014

Four Winds Press: (A division of Scholastic), 906 Sylvan Avenue, Englewood Cliffs, New Jersey 07632

Gallent Charger Publications, 34249 Camino Capistrano, Box H. Capistrano Beach, California 92624

Garrard Publishing Company, 1607 North Market Street, P.O. Box A, Champaign, Illinois 61820

GCT Publishing Co., Inc., Box 6448, Mobile, Alabama 36660

Ginn Company, P.O. Box 2649, 1250 Fairwood Avenue, Columbus, Ohio 43216

Good Apple, Inc., USPS 301-80, Box 299, Carthage, Illinois 62321

Gruner & Jahr USA Publishing, 685 Third Avenue, New York, New York 10017

Harper and Row, Inc., 10 East 53rd Street, New York, New York 10022

Hartley Courseware, Inc., 133 Bridge Street, Box 419, Dimondale, Michigan 48821

Hearst Corp., 959 Eighth Avenue, New York, New York 10021

D.C. Heath and Company, 125 Spring Street, Lexington, Massachusetts 02173

Highlights for Children, Box 269, Columbus, Ohio 43272

Holt, Rinehart, and Winston CBS, Inc., 383 Madison Avenue, New York, New York 10017

Houghton Mifflin Company, 1900 South Batavia Avenue, Geneva, Illinois 60134

Instructional Communications Technology, Inc., 10 Stepar Place, Huntington Station, New York 11746

Instructional Fair, Inc., P.O. Box 1650, Grand Rapids, Michigan 49501

The Instructor Publications, Inc. Instructor Books, 757 Third Avenue, New York, New York 10017

Intellectual Software, 798 North Avenue, Bridgeport, Connecticut 06606

Intercollegiate Video Clearinghouse, Inc., P.O. Drawer 33000R, Miami, Florida 33133

International Reading Association, 800 Barksdale Road, Newark, Delaware 19714

Jam Magazine/Ltd., 56 The Esplande, Ste. 202, Toronto, Ontario M5E1A7 Canada

Jamestown Publishers, The Reading People, P.O. box 6743, Providence, Rhode Island 02940

J/C Enterprises, Inc., 4920 Mayflower Street, Cocoa, Florida 32927

Kiplinger Washington Editors, Inc., 1729 "H" Street N.W., Washington, D.C. 20006

Laidlaw Brothers. Thatcher and Madison, River Forest, Illinois 60305

The Learning Line, P.O. Box 1200, Palo Alto, California 94302

Learning Well, 200 South Service Road, Roslyn Heights, New York 11577

Learning Periodicals Group, 19 Davis Drive, Belmont, California 94002

Learning Research Associates, P.O. Box 39, Roslyn Heights, New York 11577

Light & Life Press, 999 College Avenue, Winona Lake, Indiana 46590

Little, Brown and Company, 34 Beacon Street, Boston, Massachusetts 02106

Longman, Inc., 19 West 44th Street, New York, New York 10036

MacMillan Publishing Company, Inc., 866 Third Avenue, New York, New York 10022

Macmillan Education Ltd., Houndsmills, Basingstoke, Hampshire RG21 2XS, U.K.

Massachusetts Audubon Society, South Great Road, Lincoln, Massachusetts 01773

McGraw-Hill Book Company, 1221 Avenue of the Americas, New York, New York 10016

Charles E. Merrill Company, 1300 Alum Creek Drive, Columbus, Ohio 43216

Micro School Programs, 3647 Stone Way North, Seattle, Washington 98103

Micrograms, Inc., P.O. Box 2146, Loves Park, Illinois 61130

Micropower and Light Company, 12820 Hillcrest Road, Sutie 219, Dallas, Texas 75230

Midwest Publications, P.O. Box 448, Pacific Grove, California 93950

Milliken, 1100 Research Boulevard, P.O. Box 21579, St. Louis, Missouri 63132

Milton Bradley, 443 Shaher Road, East Longmeadow, Massachusetts 01028

Modern Curriculum Press, 13900 Prospect Road, Cleveland, Ohio 44136

Modulearn, Inc., P.O. Box 667, San Juan Capistrano, California 92693

Mutual Aid, 1953 1/2 Hillhurst Avenue, Los Angeles, California 90027

National Association of State Boards of Education, 444 North Capitol Street N.W., Washington, D.C. 20001

National Audubon Society, 950 Third Avenue, New York, New York 10022

National Geographic Society, 17th and M Street, N.W., Washington, D.C. 20036

National Wildlife Federation, Inc., 1412 Sixteenth Street N.W., Washington, D.C. 20036

New York Zoological Society, 185th Street and Southern Boulevard, Bronx, New York 10460

Nystrom Division of Carnation Co., 33033 Elston Avenue, Chicago, Illinois 60618

Open Court Publishing, P.O. Box 100, LaSalle, Illinois 61301

Opportunities for Learning, Inc., 8950 Lurline Avenue, Dept. W, Chatsworth, California 91311

Orange Cherry Media, 7 Delano Drive, Bedford Hills, Connecticut 06156

Pendulum Press, Inc., Saw Mill Road, West Haven, Connecticut 06516

Prentice-Hall, Educational Book Division, Englewood Cliffs, New Jersey 07632

Psychological Corporation, 7500 Old Oak Boulevard, Cleveland, Ohio 44130

Psychotechnics, Inc., 1900 Pickwick Avenue, Glenview, Illinois 60025

Publishers Test Service, 2500 Garden Road, Monterey, California 93940-5380

Radio Shack/Tandy Corporation, Fort Worth, Texas 76102

Rand McNally College Publishing Company, Box 7600, Chicago, Illinois 60680

Random House, School Division, 400 Hahn Road, Westminister, Massachusetts 21157

Reader's Digest Services, Inc., Educational Division, Pleasantville, New York 10570

Reading Institute, 116 Newbury Street, Boston, Massachusetts 02116

Reading Laboratory, Inc., 55 Day Street, South Norwalk, Connecticut 06854

R/C Modeler Corp., 144 West Sierra Madre Boulevard, Sierra Madre, California 91024

The Riverside Publishing Company, 8420 Bryn Mawr Avenue, Chicago, Illinois 60631

The Saturday Evening Post Co., 100 Waterway Boulevard, Box 567B, Indianapolis, Indiana 46202

Scholastic, Inc., 1290 Wall Street West, Lyndhurst, New Jersey 07071

Scienceland, 501 Fifth Avenue, New York, New York 10017

Scholastic, Inc., 904 Sylvan Avenue, Englewood Cliffs, New York 07632

Science Research Associates, Inc., 259 East Erie Street, Chicago, Illinois 60611

Scott, Foresman and Company, 1900 East Lake Avenue, Glenview, Illinois 60025

Sigma XI, The Scientific Research Society, 345 Whitney Avenue, New Haven, Connecticut 06511

Smithsonian Institution, 900 Jefferson Drive, Washington, D.C. 20560

Softside/Software, 10 Northern Boulevard, Amherst, New Hampshire 03031-2312

Special Learning Corporation, Guilford, Connecticut 06437

Spinnaker Press, Inc., Pickering Wharf, Salem, Massachusetts 01970

Society for Visual Education, Inc., 1345 Diversey Parkway, Chicago, Illinois 60614

Steck-Vaughn Company, P.O. Box 2028, Austin, Texas 78768

Sunburst Communications, Room VH-5, 39 Washington Avenue, Pleasantville, New York 10570

Teachers College Press, P.O. Box 1540, Hagerstown, Maryland 21740

T.F.H. Publications, Inc., 211 West Sylvania Avenue, Neptune City, New Jersey 07753

Troll Associates, 320 State Highway 17, Mahwah, New Jersey 07430

Two Fathoms Publishing, 2021 Brunswick Street, Suite 209B, Halifax, NS B3K 2Y5 Canada

Unity School of Christianity, Unity Village, Missouri 64065

U.S. Scholastic, Inc., 730 Broadway, New York, New York 10003

Universal Systems for Education, Inc., 195 Bonhomme Street, Hackensack, New Jersey 07602

D. Van Nostrand Company, 450 West 33rd Street, New York, New York 10001

John Wiley and Sons, Inc., 605 Third Avenue, New York, New York 10016

Winston Press, 25 Groveland Terrace, Minneapolis, Minnesota 55403

The Wright Group, 7620 Miramar Road, Suite 4200, San Diego, California 92126

Wise Owl Workshop, 1168 Avenue de las Palmas, Livermore, California 94550

World Poetry, Inc., 1616 Walnut, Room 405, Philadelphia, Pennsylvania 19103

Young Naturalist Foundation, 51 Front Street, E, Toronto, Ontario M5E1B3, Canada

Zaner-Bloser, P.O. Box 16764, Columbus, Ohio 43216-6764

Ziff Davis Publishing, 1 Park Avenue, New York, New York 10016

AUTHOR INDEX

SUBJECT INDEX

A

Anecdotal and cumulative records, 53
Autobiographies and interviews, 16

B

Background of experience, 43
Bender Visual Motor Gestalt Test, 68
Bibliotheraphy, 56
Bond and Tinker formula, 67
Brown-Carlsen Listening Comprehension Test,
  10
Bruininks-Oseretsky Test of Motor Proficiency,
  9

C

California Achievement Test, 118
California Reading Tests, 10, 86
California Test of Mental Maturity, 7
California Test of Personality, 9
Cattell Culture Fair Intelligence Test, 8
Children's Apperception Test, 9
Classroom Reading Inventory, 120
Cloze procedure, 66, 124
Competencies required, 61
Competency chart, 50
Comprehension activities, 79
Creative desk games, 57
Creative writing activities, 73
Creativity, 5
Criterion-referenced tests, 117
Cultural considerations, 48

D

Developmental Test of Visual-Motor Integration,
  9
Diagnostic procedures, 122
Diagnostic Reading Inventory, 120
Diagnostic Reading Scales, 119
Diagnostic Reading Tests, 10, 119
Differential Aptitude Tests, 9
Domain,
    affective, 106
    cognitive, 106
    perceptual, 106
Durrell Analysis of Reading Difficulty, 109,
  119

E

Emotional health, 47
Establishing programs, 26
Evaluation,
    meaning of, 110
    nature of, 102
    principles of, 108
    purposes of, 103
    utilizing results of, 125
Evolution of programs, 22
Exemplary programs, 23
Extended reading activities, 73

F

Five-step approach, 69
Frostig Program, 47
Functional reading appraisal, 52

165